# USA TODAY

# MEMORY BOOSTERS

*250 Seriously Fun Puzzles*

**Andrews McMeel**
PUBLISHING®

Andrews McMeel Publishing
a division of Andrews McMeel Universal
1130 Walnut Street, Kansas City, Missouri 64106

www.andrewsmcmeel.com

23 24 25 26 27 PAH 10 9 8 7 6 5 4 3 2 1

ISBN: 978-1-5248-8245-7

Editor: Betty Wong
Art Director: Holly Swayne
Production Editor: Brianna Westervelt
Production Manager: Julie Skalla

**ATTENTION: SCHOOLS AND BUSINESSES**

Andrews McMeel books are available at quantity discounts with bulk purchase
for educational, business, or sales promotional use. For information,
please e-mail the Andrews McMeel Publishing Special Sales Department:
sales@amuniversal.com.

# INTRODUCTION

Have you ever opened the refrigerator only to wonder why? Or see someone you've known for years and draw a blank on their name? Forgetfulness and some changes in cognitive function is a normal part of aging, one that begins when we are in our twenties. Fortunately, there are ways for people to prevent, delay, or even reverse memory decline—even for patients already struggling with Alzheimer's. One of the most important things we can do to boost our memory is to exercise our brains.

Yes, you read that right. Exercise. Exercise your body and exercise your brain.

Right now, just by reading these words, you're exercising. You're using your short-term memory to hold onto the words starting this sentence for long enough that you can get to the end and make it make sense.

(You probably haven't noticed, but that last sentence was the longest you've read so far. Did you struggle?)

Another benefit of reading is that it relies on our visual memory. Reading is often less about interpreting all the letters of a word than it is about remembering what the whole word looks like. That's true for spelling too. Children with poor visual memories often struggle to read or write because they struggle to notice that the same shape produces a different letter depending on how it's placed. A "b" is not the same as a "p."

Learning how to read is a process that takes information from our short-term memory to the long-term. And visual memory is the ability to store visual details, which will be tested by the puzzles—or brain exercises—in this book.

These puzzles start relatively easy and get progressively more tricky, so don't start at the end! Remember too, even as they get more difficult, that they're deliberately designed to make you work hard. They have to be because you're making use of your visual memory every day and it's already well developed. You navigate traffic signs, you recognize the icon on your smartphone to find your favorite podcast.

When tackling these puzzles, pay attention. Our visual memory relies on our ability to focus, and then pass these details to our short-term memory.

Our short-term memory remembers details for up to a minute. We may recall as few as four details correctly or we may remember as many as seven. So, when tackling these puzzles, be strategic. If the puzzle shows you a box made up of nine tiles, you're not going to remember all nine or their exact position. But you might remember that the tile in the top right corner is black and that the tile directly opposite (bottom left) is white.

Don't be in a rush to work through these puzzles, either. Take frequent breaks. If you try working through one after another and another, soon you'll find yourself stuck. Why? Because your brain refuses constant stimulation and needs time out—and will get it no matter what you intend. Call this your mind wandering or call it what your brain calls it: time out.

What these puzzles are doing is training you to focus your attention. The details that move into your long-term memory are the details that your short-term memory has captured successfully. An efficient short-term memory is therefore likely to enable your long-term memory to function well.

But all of us, no matter how old, have times when our short-term memory lets us down. Here's where we can blame the usual suspects: a lack of sleep, too much sugar, alcohol, or stress. A lack of sleep will make your thinking fuzzy—though, interestingly, you're more likely to trust that you're right. Alcohol disrupts the ability to retain information in the short term. Eating excessive sugar and sugary foods is linked to reduced cognitive function, including the ability to take in new knowledge and pay attention. And stress means your body has only one priority: survival. So making new memories and learning new things seems like a luxury.

Numerous studies have shown that exercise, mindfulness, and meditation is effective for reducing stress. It is also a boost for the brain, particularly for those parts of the brain associated with concentration and memory. Research has shown that meditation improves short-term memory in people of all ages.

Enjoying nature has the same effect. That may mean taking yourself for a walk or listening to a recording of sounds from nature, like running water or birdsong. Exactly why this has a positive impact is not known, but what can be measured is that it improves your ability to pay attention and also to use your memory, both short-term and long-term.

The Attention Restoration Theory may explain what's happening. The natural environment attracts our attention; we choose a focus and refuse any distraction. That makes it sound like a chore, but actually all we're doing is admiring a sunset or the golden colors of leaves in fall.

Alternatively, go socialize! Listening to your friends and engaging with what they're saying is an exercise in paying attention. And you thought you were just hanging out. But that's the thing about memory. The things helping to boost it are often the things we enjoy.

Take the same approach with these puzzles. You're not trying to pass an exam here, just have fun. Some puzzles will ask you to notice that something has moved. That's the challenge—and not whether you know what dynamic is being tested here. Form constancy, in case you were wondering; the skill of noticing that an object is the same even if its position has changed. Other puzzles will ask you to notice what's missing, and yes, it's exactly the same game that preschoolers play. It improves visual memory, which helps with reading and enhances mathematical ability—at any age.

Young or old, you'll enjoy the benefits of success. When you complete a puzzle successfully, dopamine is released, which not only enhances your mood but also increases your ability to concentrate and improves your memory. It's a virtuous circle: You're testing your memory to improve your memory.

You'll notice the benefits in other areas of your life. Memory is like a muscle, so any form of training will improve other mentally challenging activities.

So make time for yourself. And if your first thought now is that you're busy, busy, busy, are you sure you can't find even fifteen minutes today? Research has shown that just fifteen minutes of puzzling five days a week improves memory, concentration, and problem solving. Not a bad return for a total investment of just over an hour a week.

Oh, and if you want a cup of green tea or your favorite coffee before you get started, so much the better. Caffeine can boost both types of memory, short- and long-term.

WAY TO GO!

# LEVEL 1

"When I was younger I could remember anything, whether it had happened or not."
—Mark Twain

The puzzles in this section are intended as a warmup to get you used to the types of challenges you'll come across throughout the book.

## Memory Facts and Tips

When you do these puzzles, don't make any assumptions. If you are asked to study a group of playing cards, don't try to guess why. It's a funny fact that one of the ways we process information is in terms of what we expect—and that often causes us to make mistakes.

If you're new to this type of puzzle, good! Our brain thrives on new challenges. By all means enjoy a crossword or a sudoku every day, but make sure you mix in a different type of puzzle from time to time. A new puzzle is like a new language, forcing your brain to adapt.

Study the pencils below until you are familiar
with them, then turn the page.

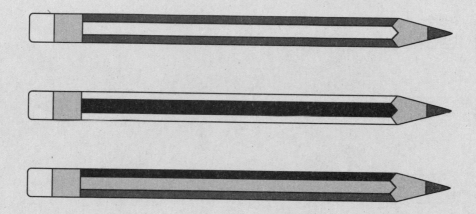

Which new pencil has appeared? When you think you have the answer, turn back the page to see if it is correct.

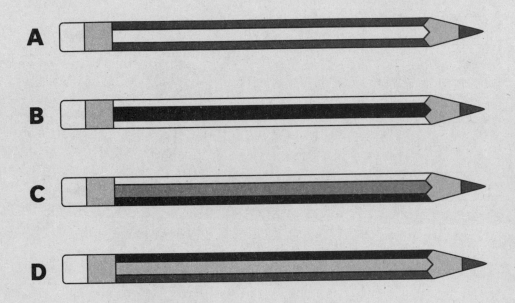

Study the cube below until you are familiar
with it, then turn the page.

Which of these did you see? When you think you have the answer, turn back the page to see if it is correct.

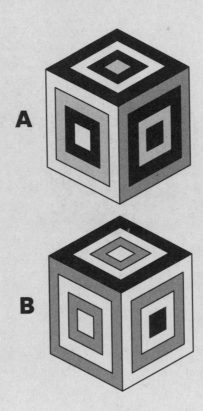

Study and memorize the fruits below, then turn the page.

BILBERRY

CLEMENTINE

ELDERBERRY

FIG

GUAVA

PASSION FRUIT

PEAR

PRUNE

RASPBERRY

SLOE

Can you find the words in the grid below? Words may run either forwards or backwards, in either a horizontal, vertical, or diagonal direction, but always in a straight line.

```
M X N Z R A S P B E R R Y
G G E B O F Z T J Y L K F
U F F N C E L E R E K V P
E E A F U G M R I E X A G
N Q P Q W R E Z R K S N O
I A G N D B P A N S A N F
T T A J R O E Q I N K D B
N L R E M P V O X K F I J
E F D D K G N C Y A L E U
M L Q M C F W N J B P M I
E O N G R J I P E B V Z M
L E L U S Q Z R W G V W Y
C W I A G L R E Q B I H O
D T Y V X Y O V Z H P F P
Y F I A E M S E E X O Q A
```

Study the tiles below until you are familiar
with them, then turn the page.

Which of these did you see? When you think you have the answer, turn back the page to see if it is correct.

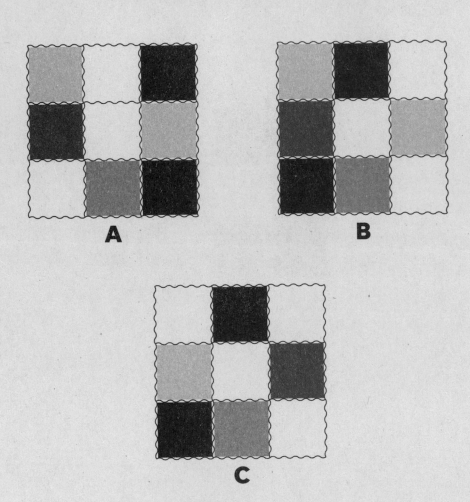

A

B

C

Study and memorize the transmission
tower below, then turn the page.

See how much you can remember about the picture.

# How many crossarms are there on the transmission tower?

# How many power lines are in the picture?

# Fewer than 10

# More than 10

# More than 15

Study the shapes below until you are familiar
with them, then turn the page.

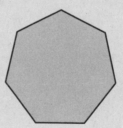

Which new shape has appeared? When you think you have the answer, turn back the page to see if it is correct.

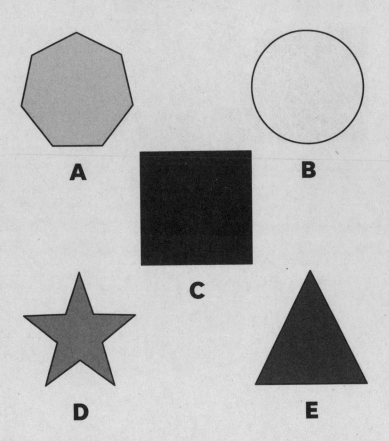

A

B

C

D

E

Study the cards below until you are familiar with them, then turn the page.

Which card is missing? When you think you have the answer, turn back the page to see if it is correct.

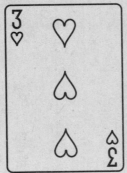

Study and memorize the list of colors below, then turn the page.

BLACK

BLUE

GREEN

INDIGO

ORANGE

PURPLE

TURQUOISE

VIOLET

WHITE

YELLOW

Can you find the words in the grid below? Words may run either forwards or backwards, in either a horizontal, vertical, or diagonal direction, but always in a straight line.

| E | C | S | L | E | I | L | I | L | J | X | F | S |
|---|---|---|---|---|---|---|---|---|---|---|---|---|
| V | D | N | T | N | K | U | N | Q | Y | B | I | P |
| B | E | A | D | V | I | O | L | E | T | I | K | R |
| S | H | I | V | E | A | Z | L | C | E | C | E | P |
| W | G | I | Y | R | C | A | L | H | W | R | H | U |
| O | B | L | A | C | K | O | J | Y | S | Y | G | K |
| A | V | J | I | E | S | I | O | U | Q | R | U | T |
| W | P | U | O | J | B | L | O | Y | V | Y | H | B |
| N | C | U | S | A | E | G | N | A | R | O | H | L |
| J | O | T | R | D | F | W | Y | M | G | E | Z | U |
| G | E | U | F | P | R | W | V | J | L | J | F | E |
| R | U | G | W | O | L | L | E | Y | Y | P | Q | K |
| O | F | D | H | R | P | E | G | A | E | E | N | D |
| P | K | X | Z | I | R | U | O | Y | I | O | Q | D |
| W | E | T | I | H | W | Z | X | G | X | Y | E | U |

Study the clock below until you are familiar
with it, then turn the page.

Which of these did you see? When you think you have the answer, turn back the page to see if it is correct.

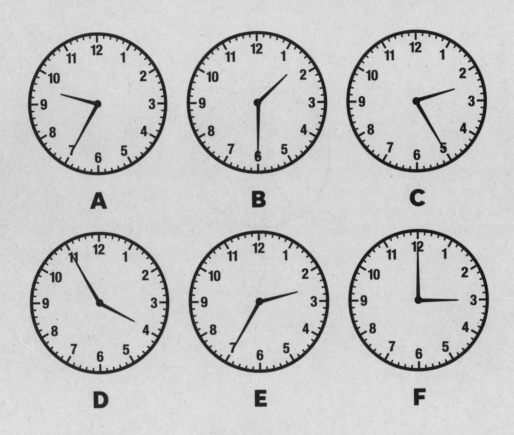

20

Study and memorize the umbrellas below, then turn the page.

See how much you can remember about the picture.

# How many umbrellas are in the image, even if only partially visible?

# How many of the umbrellas are open?

Study the beach umbrella below until you are familiar with it, then turn the page.

Which of these did you see? When you think you have the answer, turn back the page to see if it is correct.

A

B

C

Study the balloons below until you are familiar
with them, then turn the page.

Which new balloon has appeared? When you think you have the answer, turn back the page to see if it is correct.

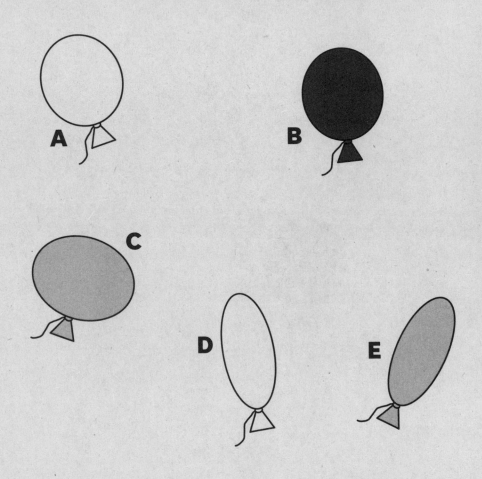

Study and memorize the list of puzzle
types below, then turn the page.

ANAGRAM

CROSSWORD

JIGSAW

LOGIC

MAZES

MEMORY

RIDDLE

SUDOKU

TANGRAM

WORD SEARCH

Can you find the words in the grid below? Words may run either forwards or backwards, in either a horizontal, vertical, or diagonal direction, but always in a straight line.

```
W S M O P I A M W G M M D
Y M A B C D N A H I T A T
T L F I J E U R R X J Z P
A W G U I J I G S A W E O
D O G D N B I N H X F S L
L W L E R P Y A T O S Z X
Z W N M O W T W Q B F O
U O C B U A W Y R O M E M
R L H C R A E S D R O W O
I E E G H V I Z S R U K S
D Y U B C T N V H O J V U
D A N A G R A M I M R Y D
L Q X P I T C A G W X C O
E U F Z X S V K H D G Y K
U Y N U D L L L U J X R U
```

Study the buttons below until you are familiar
with them, then turn the page.

Which button is different? When you think you have the answer, turn back the page to see if it is correct.

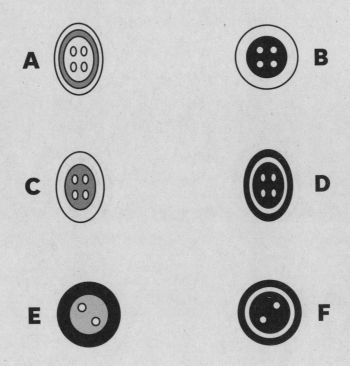

A

B

C

D

E

F

Study and memorize the chessboard below, then turn the page.

See how much you can remember about the picture.

## Are there more white or black pieces on the board?

## Which player has both rooks still in their starting positions?

## Black

## White

Study the numbers below until you are familiar
with them, then turn the page.

Which two numbers have changed shade? When you think you have the answer, turn back the page to see if it is correct.

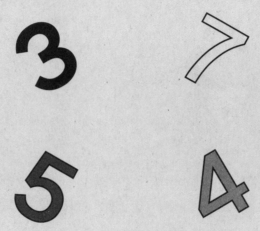

Study the building blocks below until you are
familiar with them, then turn the page.

Which one of these did you see? When you think you have the answer, turn back the page to see if it is correct.

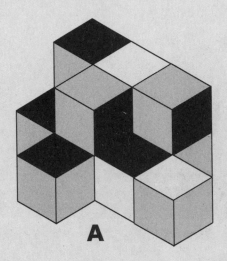

A

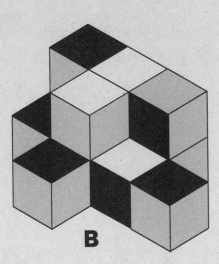

B

Study and memorize the weather words below, then turn the page.

BLIZZARD

DROUGHT

FOGGY

HEATWAVE

HURRICANE

LIGHTNING

SNOWING

SUNSHINE

TEMPERATURE

THUNDER

Can you find the words in the grid below? Words may run either forwards or backwards, in either a horizontal, vertical, or diagonal direction, but always in a straight line.

```
X Q U H M I B I Z A C B T
D J G R E D N U H T F Y K
R S U M S A O L F O G G Y
A O V P W H M I A X E X D
Z P P V I I Z G D R O I S
Z E F I K W T H U A B M H
I J N S W H P T Q H D J E
L B B I G B A N D U B B A
B C B U H R Q I H R E G T
H M O U E S D N I R N R W
I R W P B A N G T I J J A
D D M G Q I E U W C A O V
E E Q K I F Y O S A T N E
T G F B E L N T P N U C Z
O P Z R M S N S S E Q G E
```

Study the arrows below until you are familiar with them, then turn the page.

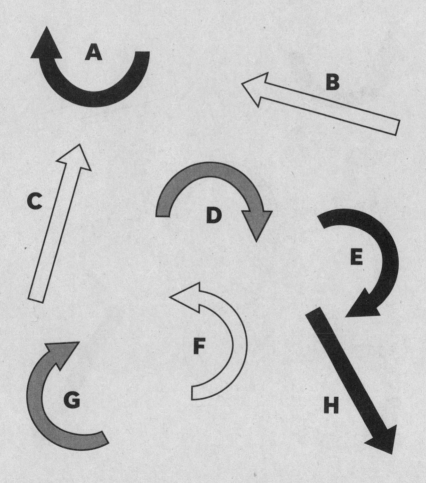

Which arrow has disappeared? When you think you have the answer, turn back the page to see if it is correct.

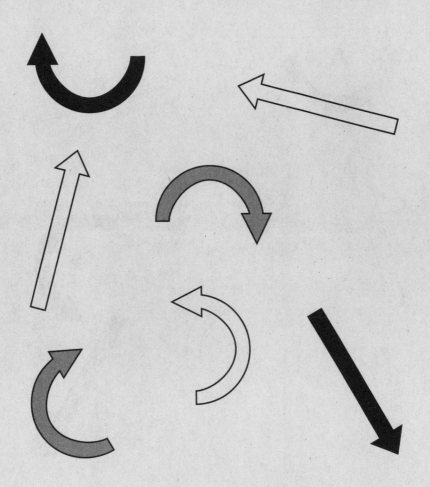

Study and memorize the Ferris wheel below, then turn the page.

See how much you can remember about the picture.

## How many cars are visible— either partially or wholly— on the Ferris wheel?

8

9

7

6

Study the designs below until you are familiar with them, then turn the page.

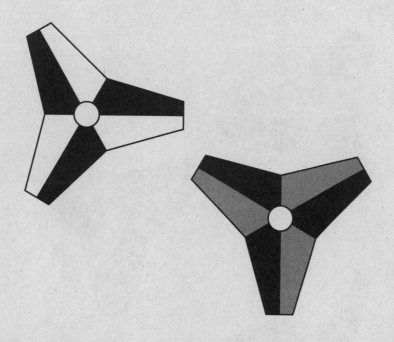

Which two of these did you see? When you think you have the answer, turn back the page to see if it is correct.

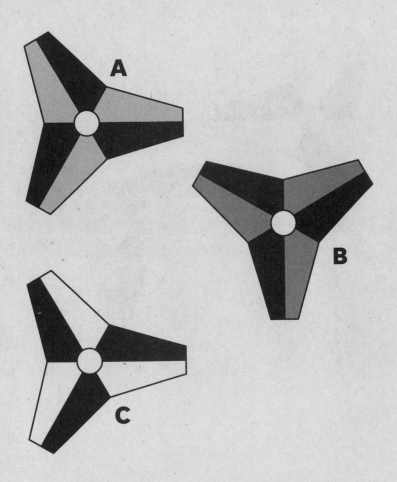

Study the hot-air balloons below until you are
familiar with them, then turn the page.

Which new hot-air balloon has appeared? When you think you have the answer, turn back the page to see if it is correct.

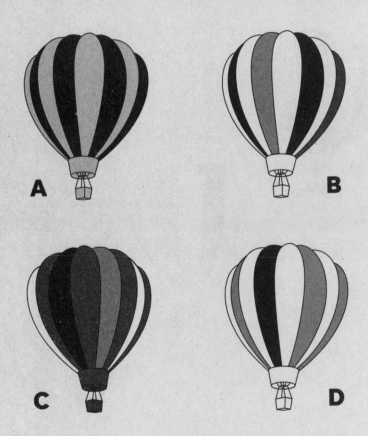

Study and memorize the toys below, then turn the page.

BARBIE DOLL

BICYCLE

FOOTBALL

PUPPET

ROCKING HORSE

SKATEBOARD

SKIPPING ROPE

TEDDY BEAR

TRAIN SET

YO-YO

Can you find the words in the grid below? Words may run either forwards or backwards, in either a horizontal, vertical, or diagonal direction, but always in a straight line.

```
R P A R A E T N T Z M B R
T Q B H U A F E Z D Z O J
I R M M X P D O R L C T S
B J A A N D J A I K G C E
U H J I Y G O C I F C U P
X A D B N B T N H P F Q O
Y N E N E S G P L J D O R
U A C T I H E W F O Y U G
R G A L O B G T X O F B N
O K N R S D N S Y R O I I
S Q S I W D H W X L A C P
R E L L A B T O O F J Y P
L L O D E I B R A B A C I
H A P Y E L V R T X E L K
T E P P U P N Z E R O E S
```

Study the house below until you are familiar
with it, then turn the page.

Which of these did you see? When you think you have the answer, turn back the page to see if it is correct.

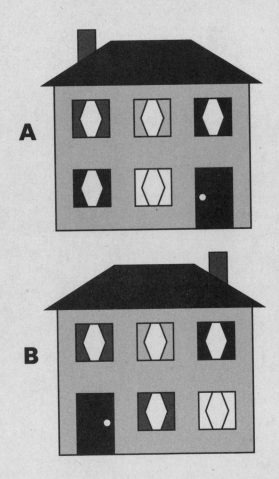

Study and memorize the ship below, then turn the page.

See how much you can remember about the picture.

# How many sails does the ship have?

# The flag of which country is being flown on the ship?

Study the board below until you are familiar
with it, then turn the page.

53

Which of these did you see? When you think you have the answer, turn back the page to see if it is correct.

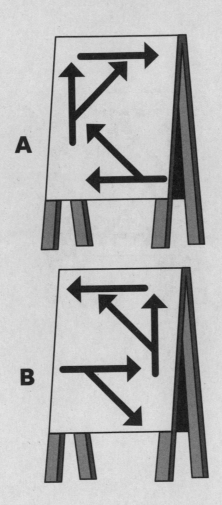

# LEVEL 2

The puzzles in this level are starting to get a bit more difficult, you'll see for example in the word search puzzles you are now asked to remember a few extra words each time!

## Memory Facts and Tips

Short-term memory is not the same as working memory. Short-term memory stores information and makes it available, while working memory can exploit that information. Short-term memory is therefore an essential function of working memory, but distinct from it.

All of the puzzles within use your short-term memory and working memory to different degrees. Some such as the word search will mostly use your short-term memory. Others such as the photographic puzzles will utilize both as you apply your working memory to the information you have absorbed using your short-term memory.

Improving our memory helps us to read—but why? The reason is that we think in terms of ideas and pictures. Improving our memory improves our ability to relate those ideas and pictures to the words we see on the page. That's why regular eye tests are so important, for children in particular. Struggling to see makes it harder to read.

Study the pencils below until you are familiar
with them, then turn the page.

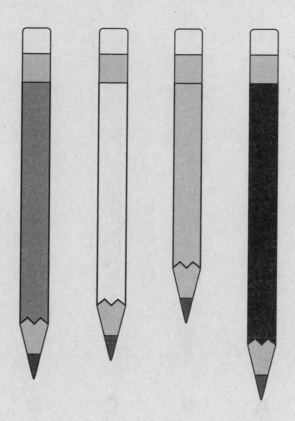

Which pencil has become shorter? When you think you have the answer, turn back the page to see if it is correct.

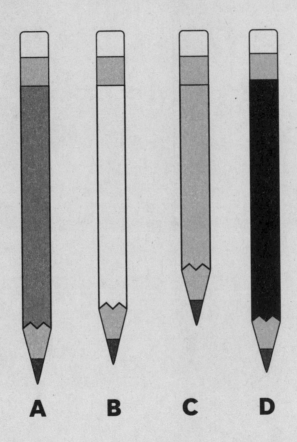

A    B    C    D

Study the cubes below until you are familiar
with them, then turn the page.

Which two of these did you see? When you think you have
the answer, turn back the page to see if it is correct.

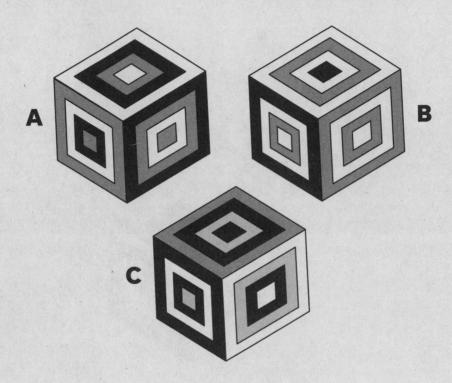

Study and memorize the gemstones below, then turn the page.

AQUAMARINE
BERYL
DIAMOND
EMERALD
GARNET
JADE
MOONSTONE
OLIVINE
OPAL
PEARL
RUBY
TOPAZ

Can you find the words in the grid below? Words may run either forwards or backwards, in either a horizontal, vertical, or diagonal direction, but always in a straight line.

```
H L Y R E B U L R A E P N
M Q T B B N I M K P U M E
N W Z E R P I H A Y F K K
T S D Y T L Y V Y J K M A
M A I K E U N S I E V O Z
J V Q J B I X R U L H O E
F Q Y U N M D R W H O N N
B W H Z A N U Y T D D S K
G N W G O M S O I J L T F
G A C M P T A R J Z A O K
F A A A A Q U R I L R N H
H I R X L B W Q I J E E G
D U L N Y O L H T N M W X
M L S W E O Z U R P E L I
Q H K N Z T O P A Z Q V Y
```

Study the tiles below until you are familiar
with them, then turn the page.

Which of these did you see? When you think you have the answer, turn back the page to see if it is correct.

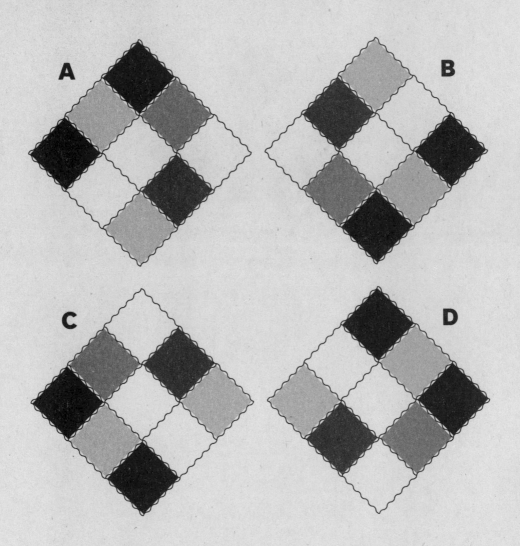

Study and memorize the chessboard below, then turn the page.

See how much you can remember about the picture.

## How many knights can you see in the image?

## Is there a king visible on the board?

Study the shapes below until you are familiar
with them, then turn the page.

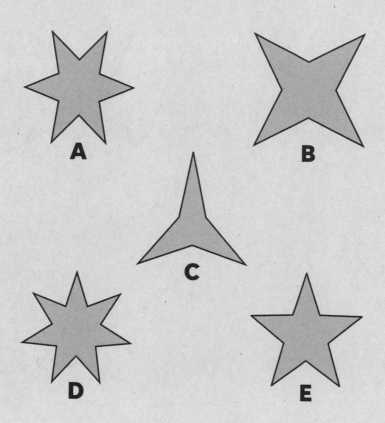

Which shape is missing? When you think you have the answer, turn back the page to see if it is correct.

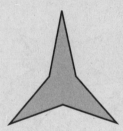

Study the cards below until you are familiar
with them, then turn the page.

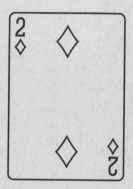

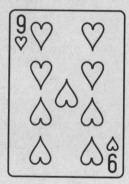

Which new card has appeared? When you think you have the answer, turn back the page to see if it is correct.

  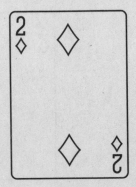

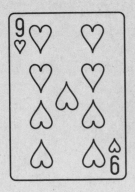  

Study and memorize the tools below, then turn the page.

CHAINSAW

CHISEL

DRILL

HAMMER

HATCHET

PLANE

PLIERS

SCRAPER

SHOVEL

SPADE

SPANNER

TWEEZERS

Can you find the words in the grid below? Words may run either forwards or backwards, in either a horizontal, vertical, or diagonal direction, but always in a straight line.

```
J N I Q Q Y B V H Y K M K
Y G I Z R E M M A H A B N
B D C Q B E C U W C E Q D
K B T W C U N L E V O H S
I R C W Q H X J Q N G I R
B T N D E H A T J P C A L
T E J D K E K I N O C A E
R H L L Z M Z R N D A R S
E C N K S S V E R S E U I
P T V Q E W R I R N A Y H
A A G D V R L E N S N W C
R H A X A L U A I O S H Z
C P H I N Q P G G L J S R
S E T I N S E N A L P G E
U R W O X I X K Q G T Y M
```

Study the clocks below until you are familiar
with them, then turn the page.

Which two of these did you see? When you think you have the answer, turn back the page to see if it is correct.

Study and memorize the Eiffel Tower below, then turn the page.

See how much you can remember about the picture.

## How many bridge arches can be seen in the image?

## What can be seen at the bottom right of the Eiffel Tower?

Study the beach umbrellas below until you are familiar with them, then turn the page.

Which new beach umbrella has appeared? When you think you have the answer, turn back the page to see if it is correct.

Study the balloons below until you are familiar
with them, then turn the page.

Which balloon has disappeared? When you think you have the answer, turn back the page to see if it is correct.

Study and memorize the birds below, then turn the page.

BUZZARD
CANARY
EAGLE
FLAMINGO
GOOSE
OSTRICH
PARROT
PIGEON
ROBIN
STARLING
TURKEY
VULTURE

Can you find the words in the grid below? Words may run either forwards or backwards, in either a horizontal, vertical, or diagonal direction, but always in a straight line.

```
E J S G N I L R A T S A N
V C M Z X G L Z H E X I F
F L A M I N G O R V B G J
P M H R Q S D U M O A K G
I M Y A P R T E R A I P O
P U M K A L Y M L L T S L
Y S U Z U W Z C S P T X P
M R Z V Z H Z L T R I M A
E U A Q Z B T U I Y C Q R
B U D N R N R C I D E M R
X R T V A K H E J R G Y O
O Y F U E C S H A O T T T
I Z H Y D G B Z O G W T P
D M H Q C H Y S A Q L N A
S R Y Z N O E G I P K E B
```

Study the buttons below until you are familiar
with them, then turn the page.

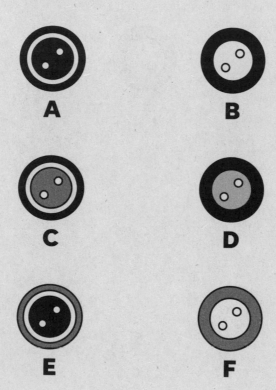

Which button is missing? When you think you have the answer, turn back the page to see if it is correct.

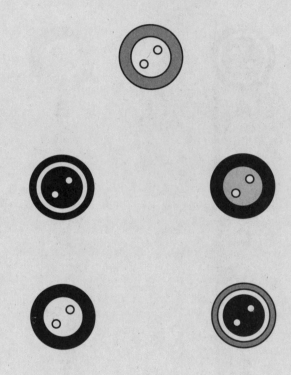

Study and memorize the telephone keypad
below, then turn the page.

See how much you can remember about the picture.

## What letters appear on the 5 key?

**GHI**

**JKL**

**PRS**

**DEF**

Study the letters below until you are familiar with them, then turn the page.

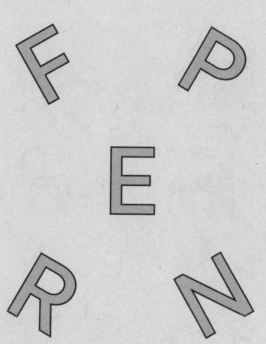

Which new letter has appeared? When you think you have the answer, turn back the page to see if it is correct.

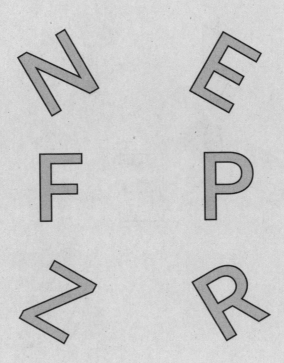

Study the building blocks below until you are
familiar with them, then turn the page.

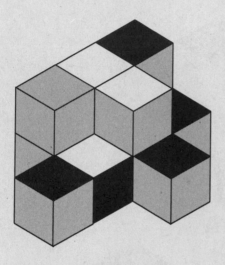

Which one of these did you NOT see? When you think you have the answer, turn back the page to see if it is correct.

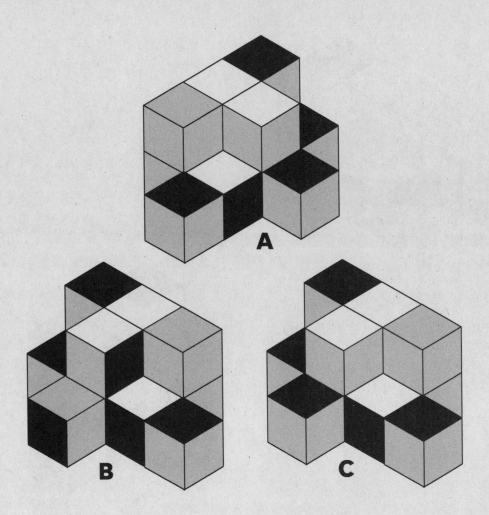

A

B

C

Study and memorize the types of cakes below, then turn the page.

BIRTHDAY

BROWNIES

CHERRY

CHOCOLATE

CHRISTMAS

COCONUT

COFFEE

FRUIT

GINGER

LAYER

MUFFIN

WEDDING

Can you find the words in the grid below? Words may run either forwards or backwards, in either a horizontal, vertical, or diagonal direction, but always in a straight line.

```
L B S X P X M I F R U I T
F K C Y A D H T R I B K M
H T H H T K R C U W R A E
M P R G S F P E I B Q Z C
P A I L J W N N G F T O A
E L S W E M B N I N F D P
T L T N W O I C M F I N I
A L M Z B D O O E G F G W
L A A I D C E E L U D U Y
O Y S E O P Q B E M T O M
C E W N B Y N Q A I H G P
O R U B S S E I N W O R B
H T B A W B P Y T T E W B
C V J I L H N C H E R R Y
H W C P J L B U Q V H J K
```

Study the arrows below until you are familiar
with them, then turn the page.

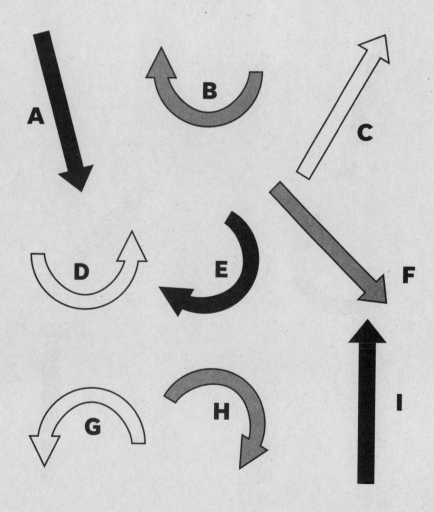

USA TODAY

Which two arrows have changed places? When you think you have the answer, turn back the page to see if it is correct.

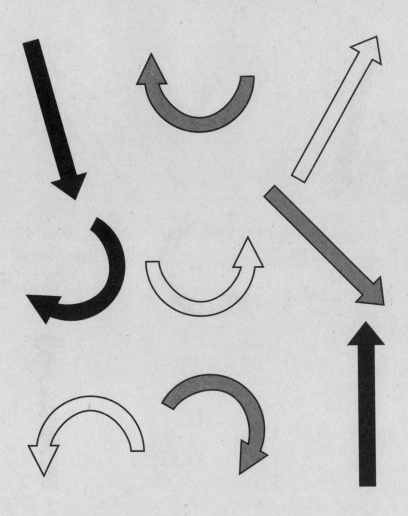

Study and memorize the bus stop image below, then turn the page.

See how much you can remember about the picture.

## Where would you be going if you caught the Q32 bus?

## Jackson Heights

## The Cloisters

## Madison Av & E 49 St

Study the designs below until you are familiar
with them, then turn the page.

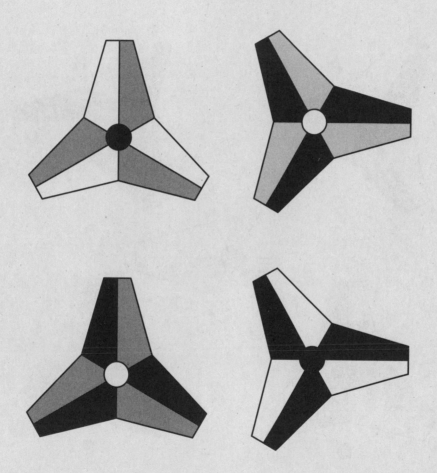

Which new design has appeared? When you think you have the answer, turn back the page to see if it is correct.

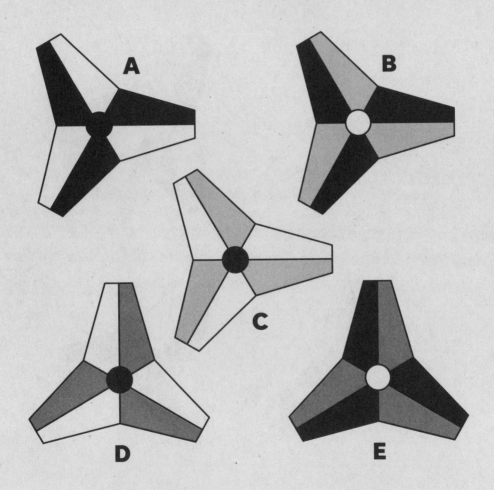

Study the hot-air balloons below until you are familiar with them, then turn the page.

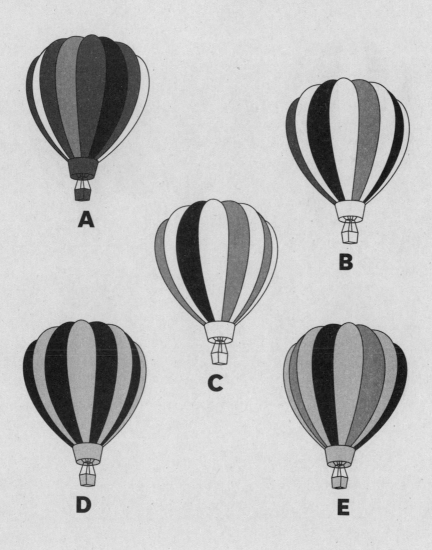

Which hot-air balloon is missing? When you think you have the answer, turn back the page to see if it is correct.

Study and memorize the items of clothing
below, then turn the page.

GLOVES

JACKET

JEANS

MITTENS

NECK SCARF

PANTS

PINAFORE

SARI

SHORTS

SKIRT

SWEATER

TUXEDO

Can you find the words in the grid below? Words may run either forwards or backwards, in either a horizontal, vertical, or diagonal direction, but always in a straight line.

| | | | | | | | | | | | |
|---|---|---|---|---|---|---|---|---|---|---|---|
| T | M | G | J | C | E | M | D | L | O | E | Y | Y |
| A | R | M | U | Y | Q | G | D | N | I | A | L | W |
| T | H | I | K | I | G | E | Q | Z | P | R | M | P |
| F | U | I | K | Z | C | H | T | E | K | C | A | J |
| R | Q | X | W | S | U | B | T | D | Q | N | H | S |
| A | D | R | E | R | Y | Z | A | C | T | V | S | M |
| C | K | U | D | D | J | Z | E | S | X | Z | E | I |
| S | Z | U | B | Y | O | R | U | W | C | Z | V | T |
| K | K | W | B | U | O | Z | K | J | T | P | O | T |
| C | S | T | A | F | Q | B | E | I | E | F | L | E |
| E | S | H | A | A | J | P | M | U | A | A | G | N |
| N | V | N | O | R | Y | W | F | O | M | U | N | S |
| J | I | Q | L | R | U | A | Y | S | C | Z | H | S |
| P | K | R | R | E | T | A | E | W | S | M | F | G |
| J | U | R | A | G | X | S | C | T | X | Z | Q | S |

Study the houses below until you are familiar
with them, then turn the page.

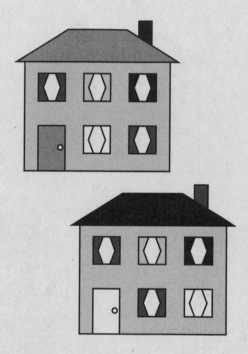

Which new house has appeared? When you think you have the answer, turn back the page to see if it is correct.

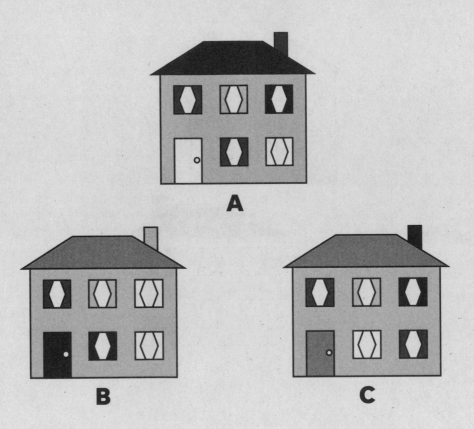

Study and memorize the juggling picture
below, then turn the page.

See how much you can remember about the picture.

## How many pieces of fruit are in the image?

4

7

8

5

6

Study the board below until you are familiar
with it, then turn the page.

Which of these did you see? When you think you have the answer, turn back the page to see if it is correct.

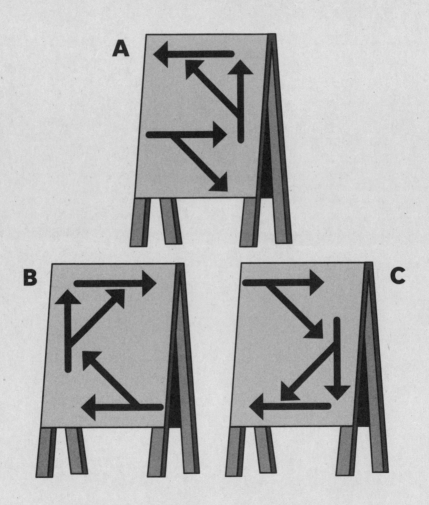

# LEVEL 3

> "If you wish to forget anything on the spot, make a note that this thing is to be remembered."
>
> —Edgar Allan Poe

Welcome to level 3. Now things are starting to get a bit trickier, but if you've worked your way through levels 1 and 2 you should be strengthening your skills and getting better as you go!

## Memory Facts and Tips

Photographic memory doesn't exist. At least, not the way we think about it, as if our memory is like a photograph we can examine whenever we want. What we do all have is a developed visual memory, which is why most of us are more likely to remember a face than a name.

Embrace mindfulness. Bringing your attention to the present moment without judgment lowers stress and improves working memory and the ability to concentrate, which are both key to forming long-term memories. There are many ways to practice mindfulness. You can be fully present anywhere, at any time, no matter what you are doing. Just set aside ten to twelve minutes every day and stick with it.

Study the pencils below until you are familiar
with them, then turn the page.

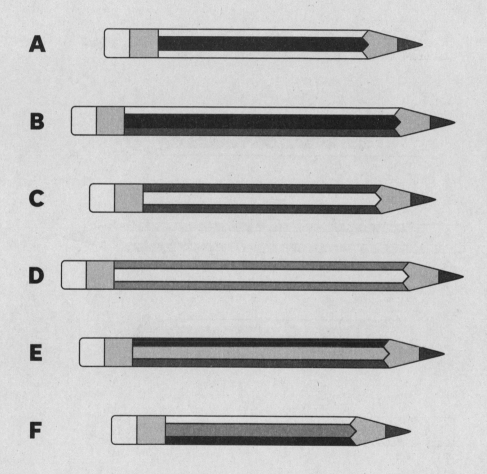

Which pencil is missing? When you think you have the answer, turn back the page to see if it is correct.

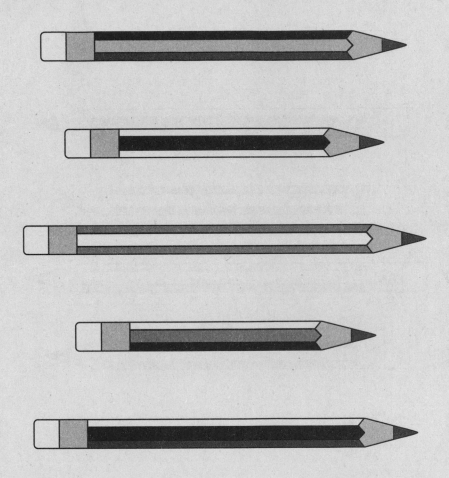

Study the cubes below until you are familiar
with them, then turn the page.

Which new cube has appeared? When you think you have the answer, turn back the page to see if it is correct.

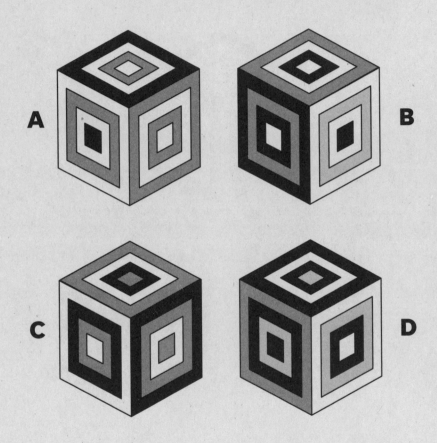

Study and memorize the European countries
below, then turn the page.

CROATIA

FRANCE

GERMANY

GREECE

ITALY

LIECHTENSTEIN

LITHUANIA

MALTA

NORWAY

PORTUGAL

ROMANIA

SERBIA

SLOVENIA

SPAIN

Can you find the words in the grid below? Words may run either forwards or backwards, in either a horizontal, vertical, or diagonal direction, but always in a straight line.

```
Y H L E S A I N A M O R E
N M R A V E R L A K P W Z
A O K W C B S E W Y A N B
M U R E J R M N W I I I A
R K E W A V O W N A L E I
E R I Y A P E A P S E T N
G W E R E Y U S T X A S E
L N C A O H U A W I Y N V
A G Z E T W E I A B A E O
O Y J I Z O C B L U S T L
M A L T A Z N R L D O H S
S E M A T I A E A O R C E
D M L E T K R S N A T E N
E L A T S I F X D F C I D
L A G U T R O P A N D L I
```

Study the two sets of tiles below until you are familiar with them, then turn the page.

Which two of these did you see? When you think you have the answer, turn back the page to see if it is correct.

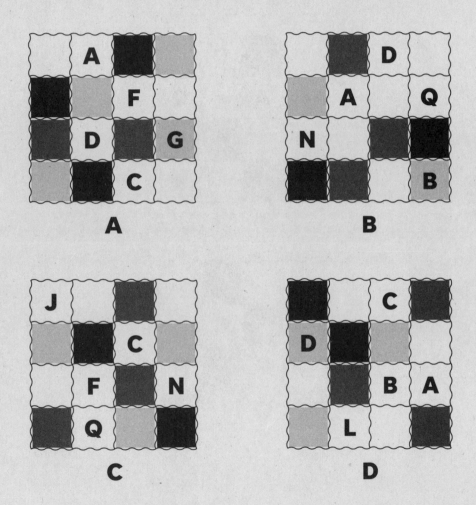

A

B

C

D

Study and memorize the fish market image
below, then turn the page.

See how much you can remember about the picture.

# Which two prices are not displayed?

5.80

4.40

5.60

2.00

5.40

4.20

Study the shapes below until you are familiar
with them, then turn the page.

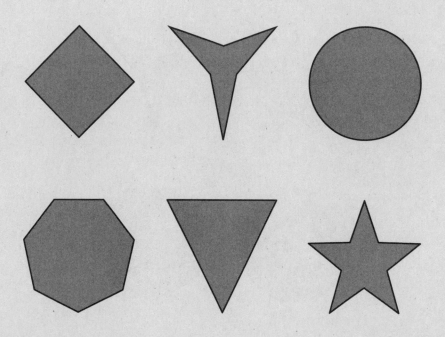

Which new shape has appeared? When you think you have the answer, turn back the page to see if it is correct.

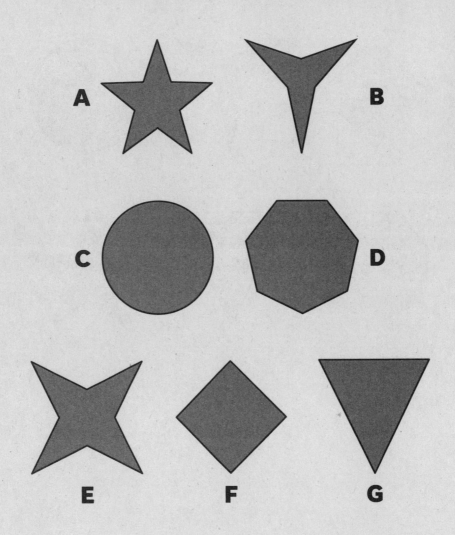

Study the cards below until you are familiar
with them, then turn the page.

Which card has changed suit? When you think you have the answer, turn back the page to see if it is correct.

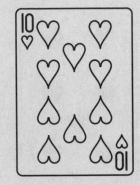

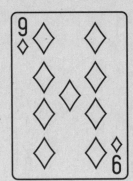

Study and memorize the wild flowers below, then turn the page.

ANEMONE

BLUEBELL

BUTTERCUP

CLOVER

CORNFLOWER

DAISY

DANDELION

FOXGLOVE

HEATHER

ORCHID

POISON IVY

POPPY

SNOWDROP

THISTLE

Can you find the words in the grid below? Words may run either forwards or backwards, in either a horizontal, vertical, or diagonal direction, but always in a straight line.

```
Y L M P P Y V C P R G B P
P D M U S B T W E U R B Y
U Y R I R Z K H A A E C P
C E A G R U T R N M W U P
R D L P D A P O P M O C O
E N W T E M I R T N L Q P
T L A H S L K G D O F S P
T H R N E I N Z V D N O O
U P T D O Y H E L S R L I
B K N V C L R T J D O O S
P A D I H C R O W T C Z O
D E V O L G X O F W W F N
F A N E M O N E T V G R I
P E H R K S H X C D K M V
E D B L U E B E L L Y L Y
```

Study the clocks below until you are familiar
with them, then turn the page.

USA TODAY

Which clock is showing a different time? When you think you
have the answer, turn back the page to see if it is correct.

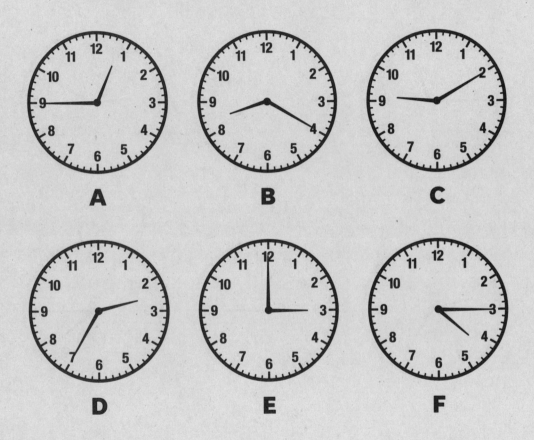

A       B       C

D       E       F

Study and memorize the bridge below, then turn the page.

See how much you can remember about the picture.

## How many lanterns light the bridge?

## What is attached to the bridge?

Study the beach umbrellas below until you are familiar with them, then turn the page.

Which two have changed places? When you think you have the answer, turn back the page to see if it is correct.

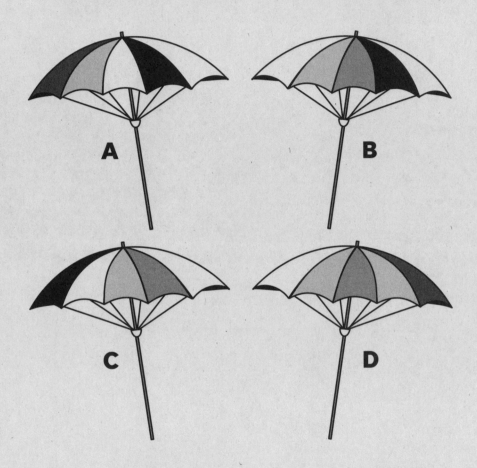

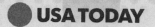
Study the balloons below until you are familiar with them, then turn the page.

Which balloon has changed position? When you think you have the answer, turn back the page to see if it is correct.

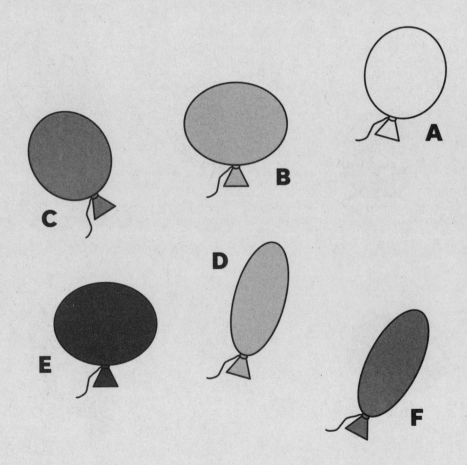

Study and memorize the cat breeds below, then turn the page.

ABYSSINIAN

BALINESE

BENGAL

BIRMAN

BURMESE

DEVON REX

MAINE COON

MANX

PERSIAN

RAGDOLL

SIAMESE

SIBERIAN

SOKOKE

TURKISH VAN

Can you find the words in the grid below? Words may run either forwards or backwards, in either a horizontal, vertical, or diagonal direction, but always in a straight line.

```
N O O C E N I A M W N A W
T Y O B G P A B U A A D N
A U Q U I X U X I Y M L C
F U R X E R M R W X V A O
E A U K M K E G E X N G N
S G B E I B O R T U A N A
E M S Y I S N K B A I E M
M E O S S O H A O V S B R
A J H U V S L V C S R W I
I Z M E J I I V A A E R B
S N D I N D P N G N P A H
V A Y E K G J D I E M R I
C L S Z S Z O R W A K S F
Y E Q B J L V S N D N T O
C O N F L P E X I P G A G
```

Study the buttons below until you are familiar
with them, then turn the page.

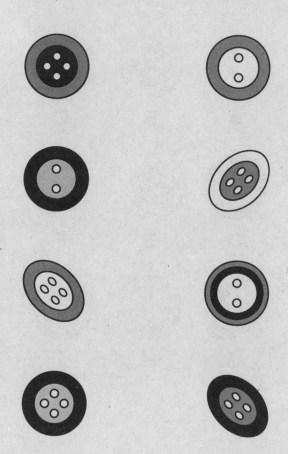

Which new button has appeared? When you think you have the answer, turn back the page to see if it is correct.

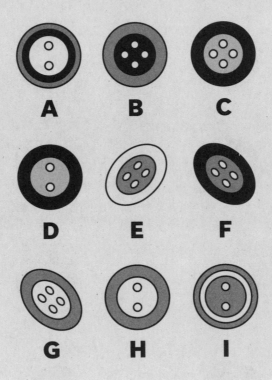

A          B          C

D          E          F

G          H          I

Study and memorize the warehouse below, then turn the page.

See how much you can remember about the picture.

## How many stacks high are the barrels at their highest point?

7

5

6

8

Study the numbers below until you are familiar
with them, then turn the page.

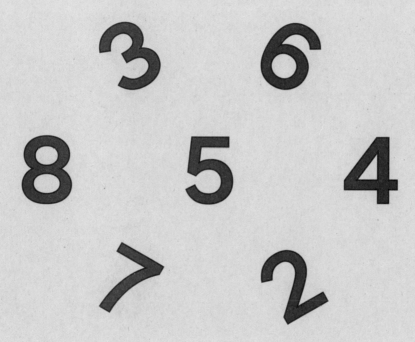

What number has disappeared? When you think you have the answer, turn back the page to see if it is correct.

5

2

7

6

3

8

Study the building blocks below until you are familiar with them, then turn the page.

Which one of these did you see? When you think you have the answer, turn back the page to see if it is correct.

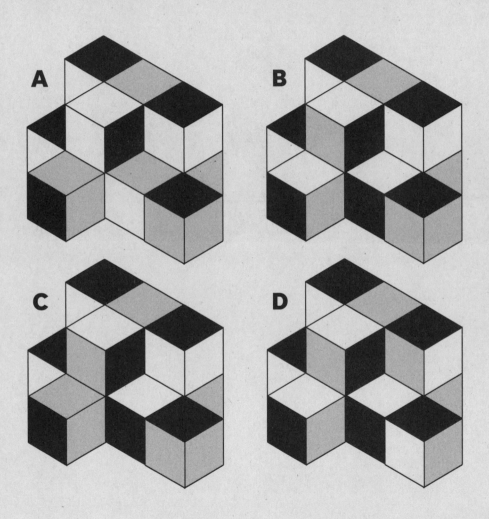

Study and memorize the animals below, then turn the page.

BEAVER

COYOTE

CROCODILE

ELEPHANT

HIPPOPOTAMUS

KANGAROO

LYNX

MONKEY

MOOSE

RABBIT

RACCOON

RHINOCEROS

TIGER

WOLF

Can you find the words in the grid below? Words may run either forwards or backwards, in either a horizontal, vertical, or diagonal direction, but always in a straight line.

```
O O B Z G S K S K R R Z R
Y E K N O M G Y W A H L U
C Y W E U O S L M O I Z U
R M B Z L Q B T S O N O B
O Q S Q V D N E U J O O Q
C G V K G A R V M R C S V
O I C C H E J N A T E A E
D L U P V M C G T R R J M
I C E A K T N G O T O R M
L L E E I A F F P C S A F
E B T B K L E T O Y O C L
R C B I O L R P P U O C Y
Z A Q W G M B H P J O O N
R M D Q C E R V I B X O X
P U Z P A G R A H V Y N O
```

Study the arrows below until you are familiar
with them, then turn the page.

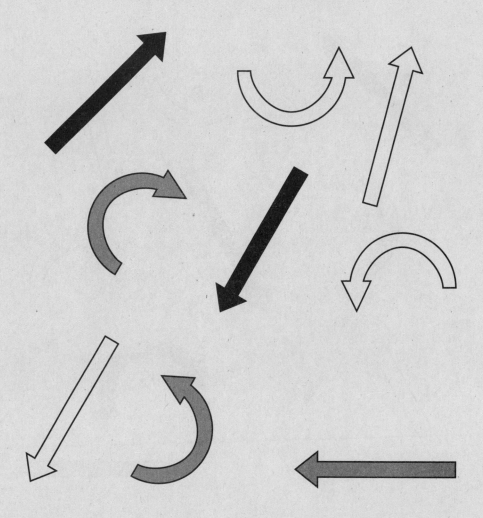

Which new arrow has appeared? When you think you have the answer, turn back the page to see if it is correct.

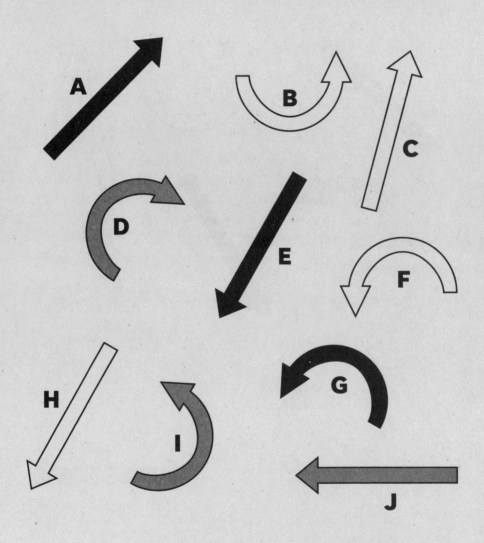

Study and memorize the castle gate below, then turn the page.

See how much you can remember about the picture.

# How many square holes are there in the closed part of the gate?

32

24

30

36

22

Study the designs below until you are familiar
with them, then turn the page.

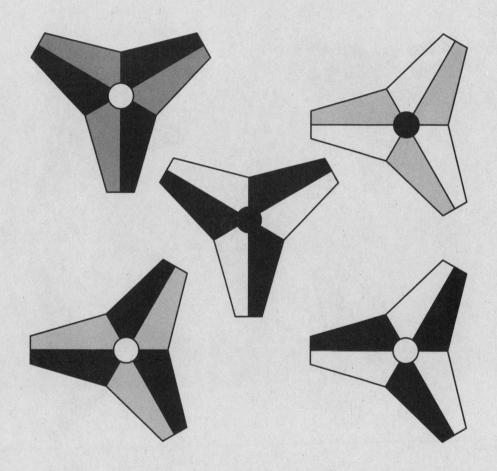

Which two designs have changed places? When you think you have the answer, turn back the page to see if it is correct.

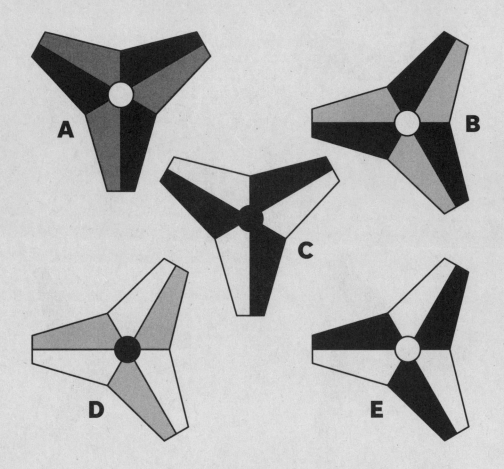

A

B

C

D

E

Study the hot-air balloons below until you are familiar with them, then turn the page.

Which new hot-air balloon has appeared? When you think you have the answer, turn back the page to see if it is correct.

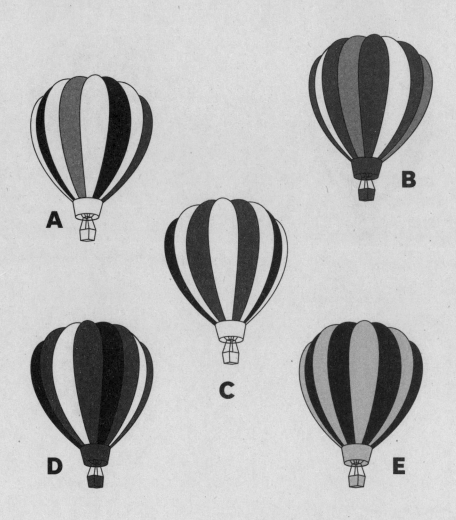

Study and memorize the desserts below, then turn the page.

APPLE PIE

BAKED ALASKA

BAKLAVA

CHEESECAKE

COBBLER

ICE CREAM

MOUSSE

PARFAIT

PAVLOVA

SORBET

SOUFFLE

SUNDAE

SYLLABUB

TIRAMISU

Can you find the words in the grid below? Words may run either forwards or backwards, in either a horizontal, vertical, or diagonal direction, but always in a straight line.

```
A F M G M B B C P U H E A
P C N O O A S K S Q G Z N
P C A E K K X I H Q S V N
L H F L A L M Z K R U N B
E E X L S A P S U N D A E
P E N S R V P R R F K Y N
I S A I H A M O D E A M L
E E T V A S T O D M B A S
I C J V O I O A U R B E Y
P A L R A L L L E S L R L
I K B F W A V L R F S C L
B E R M S Y B A F H G E A
T A A K F B F U P F Q C B
P D A D O J O H C S Z I U
O R J C V S E B D R J T B
```

Study the houses below until you are familiar with them, then turn the page.

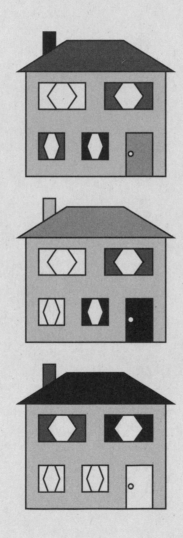

Which house has had its door repainted? When you think you have the answer, turn back the page to see if it is correct.

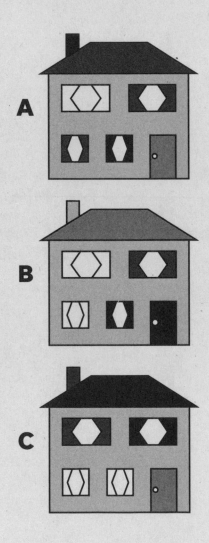

Study and memorize the sale below, then turn the page.

See how much you can remember about the picture.

## Which of the following two statements do not appear on any sign in the store?

**ANY GARMENT ON THIS RACK $25.55**

**NO ALTERATIONS**

**ANY GARMENT ON THIS RACK $9.99**

**ANY GARMENT ON THIS RACK $24.44**

**NO EXCHANGES**

**NO EXIT**

**EVERY SALE FINAL**

Study the boards below until you are familiar
with them, then turn the page.

Which new board has appeared? When you think you have the answer, turn back the page to see if it is correct.

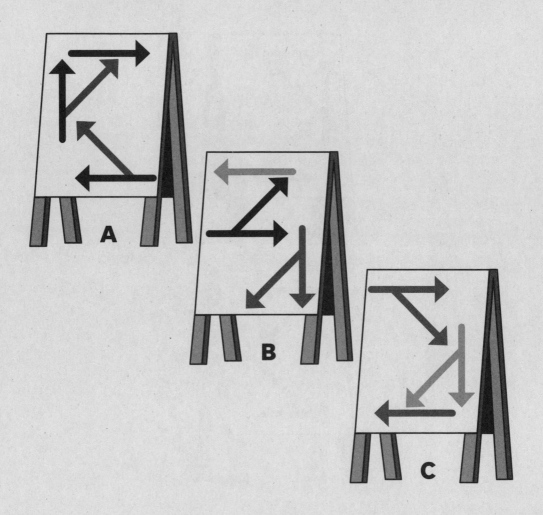

# LEVEL 4

"If a brain is exercised properly, anyone can grow intelligence, at any age, and potentially by a lot. Or you can just let your brain idle—and watch it slowly, inexorably, go to seed like a sedentary body."

—Michael Merzenich, neuroscientist and professor emeritus UCSF

In level 4 you'll really start to be tested. You'll notice that the number of options to choose between in the visual puzzles continues to increase, really challenging your skills of observation!

## Memory Facts and Tips

If you're worried about your memory, check in with others who know you well. If your friends and your family don't see a problem, then chances are there isn't one. We've all looked for our keys at some point, we've all forgotten a word. We're all getting older and occasionally draw a blank. Don't sweat it.

One simple everyday method of putting your memory to the test is to write out your grocery list with pen and paper. Then attempt to remember all items on the list without referring to it. Once you think you have everything that you listed, compare it to the physical list and see how you did. Writing something out by hand on physical paper tends to trigger more brain activity and allows us to retain information better. Try jotting down important notes and lists the old-fashioned way to help your memorization.

Study the pencils below until you are familiar
with them, then turn the page.

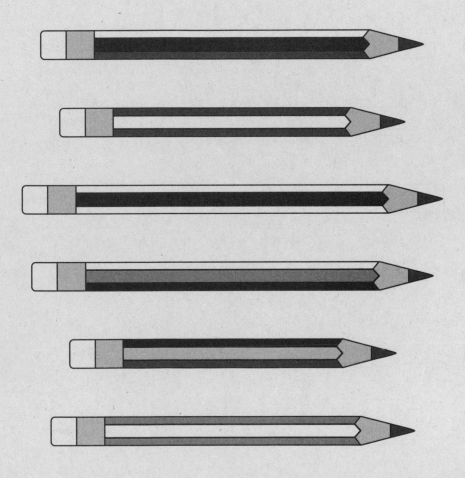

Which two pencils have changed places? When you think you have the answer, turn back the page to see if it is correct.

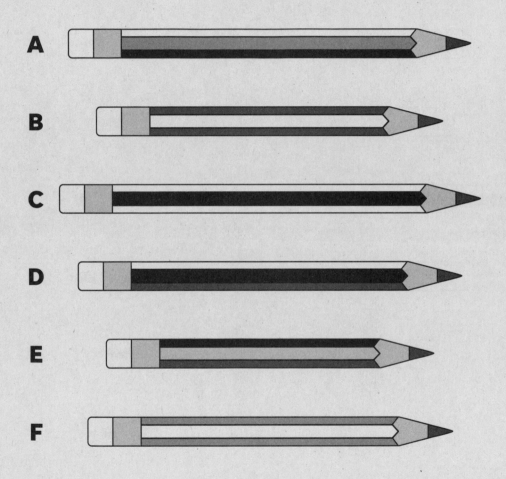

Study the cubes below until you are familiar
with them, then turn the page.

Which cube is missing? When you think you have the answer, turn back the page to see if it is correct.

Study and memorize the states below, then turn the page.

| | |
|---|---|
| ALABAMA | OREGON |
| GEORGIA | RHODE ISLAND |
| IDAHO | TEXAS |
| IOWA | UTAH |
| MAINE | VERMONT |
| MARYLAND | WEST VIRGINIA |
| NEW JERSEY | WISCONSIN |
| OHIO | WYOMING |

Can you find the words in the grid below? Words may run either forwards or backwards, in either a horizontal, vertical, or diagonal direction, but always in a straight line.

```
A M A B A L A S A G D T A
I B D A T E X A L N H I L
N I W Y O M I W A A N H A
E O V D W I K L A I U F S
I N I D D G S X G M P V K
N L I A N I J R H A T U N
E O H A E A I D I A V O Z
W O I D M V L L E S G R W
J T O H T A S Y R E Z V A
E H P S O Z W A R C S E I
R S E N E W J O X A G R G
S W Y O M I N G J E M M R
E A G E O R A I G F T O O
Y A R E G O N I A T A N E
B K N I S N O C S I W T G
```

170

Study the tiles below until you are familiar
with them, then turn the page.

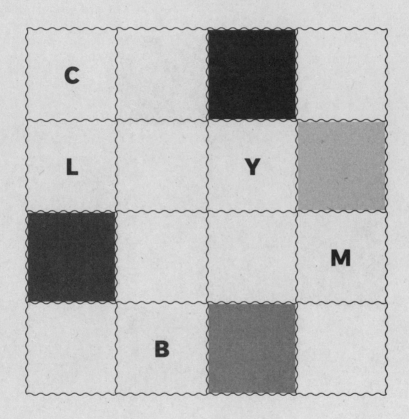

Write in the missing letters, then turn back the
page to see if your answer is correct.

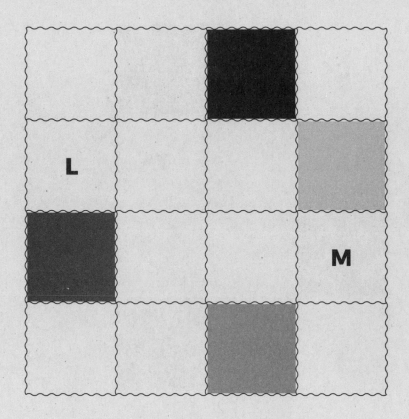

Study and memorize the palm trees below, then turn the page.

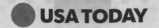

See how much you can remember about the picture.

## How many palm trees can be seen on the traffic island in the foreground?

## Are there any vehicles in the image?

Study the shapes below until you are familiar with them, then turn the page.

Which two shapes have changed places? When you think you have the answer, turn back the page to see if it is correct.

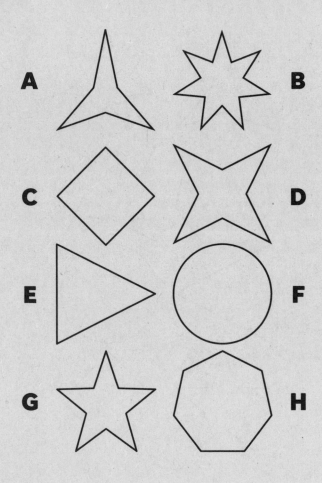

Study the cards below until you are familiar
with them, then turn the page.

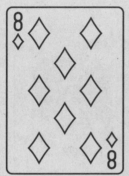

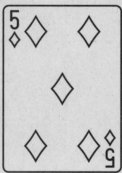

Which playing card is missing? When you think you have the answer, turn back the page to see if it is correct.

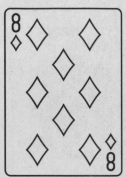  

Study and memorize the list of shells below, then turn the page.

| | |
|---|---|
| ABALONE | MUSSEL |
| AMMONITE | NAUTILUS |
| CLAM | OYSTER |
| CONCH | RAZOR |
| COWRIE | SCALLOP |
| HORNSHELL | SNAIL |
| LIMPET | TURTLE |
| MUREX | WHELK |

Can you find the words in the grid below? Words may run either forwards or backwards, in either a horizontal, vertical, or diagonal direction, but always in a straight line.

```
E P G X N J P Y O T W S E
M N I K Q O A R J H T N Z
W A C T L D Q F E L O O X
X Z L L U D K L H L O D C
K R A C S R K Q A S Z O O
P C Z N Y M T B L U T B N
S G A U R U A L L L E L C
V I G I X S S Z E I P E H
L O R E T S Y O H T M T J
M I Z J Z E V X S U I I C
R N D U G L Z M N A L N O
L A N B O S U U R N Y O W
B W Z R P R D S O P V M R
V Z J O E C C Q H J H M I
X P R X R J R J G D Z A E
```

Study the clocks below until you are familiar
with them, then turn the page.

Which three of these did you see? When you think you have the answer, turn back the page to see if it is correct.

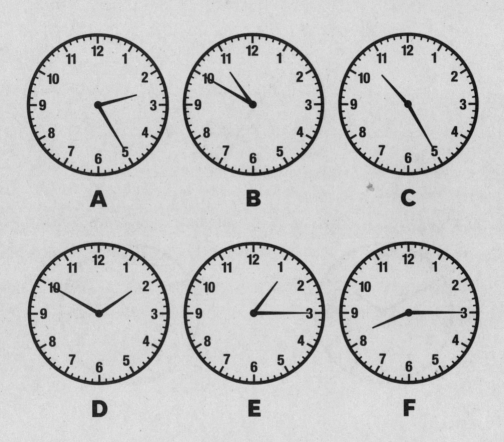

Study and memorize the harbor below, then turn the page.

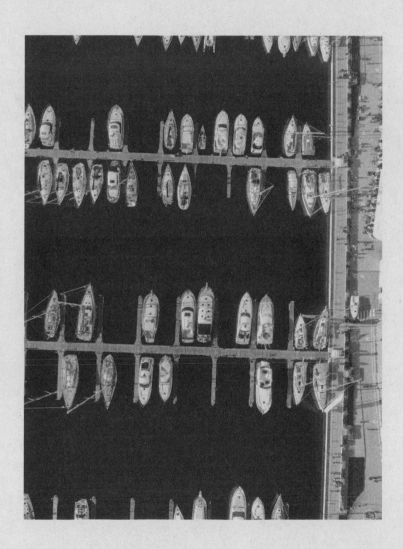

See how much you can remember about the picture.

# If you imagine a horizontal line across the image, how many water vessels can you see in their entirety in the bottom section?

Study the beach umbrellas below until you are familiar with them, then turn the page.

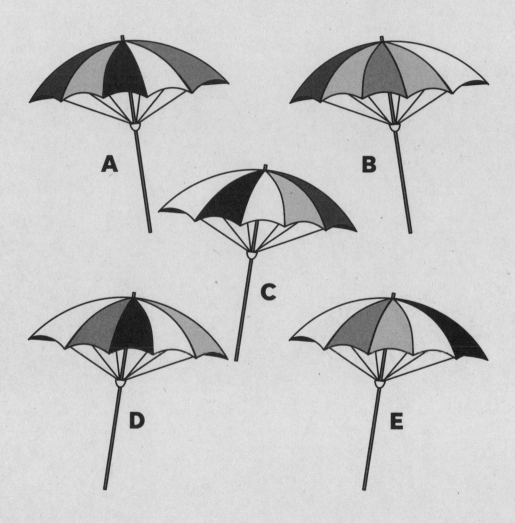

Which umbrella is missing? When you think you have the
answer, turn back the page to see if it is correct.

Study the balloons below until you are familiar
with them, then turn the page.

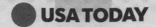

Which two balloons have changed places? When you think you have the answer, turn back the page to see if it is correct.

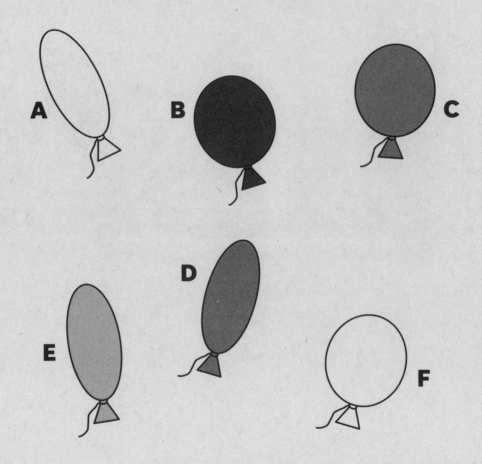

Study and memorize the dances below, then turn the page.

| | |
|---|---|
| BEGUINE | MOONWALK |
| BOLERO | POLKA |
| CHARLESTON | RUMBA |
| FANDANGO | SAMBA |
| FLAMENCO | TANGO |
| JIVE | TARANTELLA |
| LINDY HOP | TWIST |
| MAMBO | WALTZ |

Can you find the words in the grid below? Words may run either forwards or backwards, in either a horizontal, vertical, or diagonal direction, but always in a straight line.

```
L V L F V S H E T E S M M
T S I W T B R W K Y O D O
E V I J P E T X A G G U O
O Y K O S G T A N L B A N
O Z L O H U U A N I T O W
T K A X C I D Q O G T Z A
A O H V E N A C W S O O L
R M U Q A E N B E J O C K
A H M F D E X L M I T M H
N I E A M S R Z X U G L O
T D P A M A A E J D R R U
E B L I H B N M L A E V U
L F C C T M O A B L K B B
L I N D Y H O P O A Y F U
A X S B Y M V B L X F K P
```

Study the buttons below until you are familiar
with them, then turn the page.

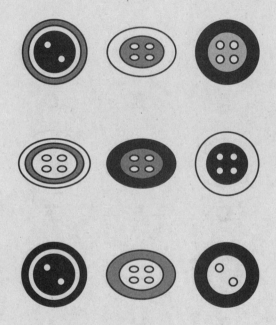

Which two buttons have changed places? When you think you have the answer, turn back the page to see if it is correct.

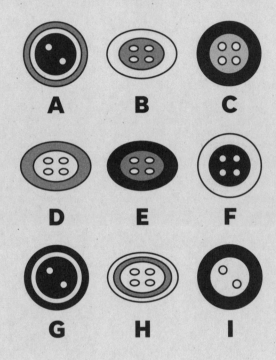

Study and memorize the columns below, then turn the page.

See how much you can remember about the picture.

# Can you see the shadow of every column?

Study the letters below until you are familiar
with them, then turn the page.

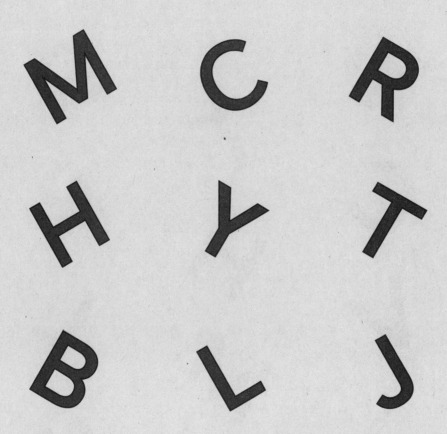

Which two new letters have appeared? When you think you have the answer, turn back the page to see if it is correct.

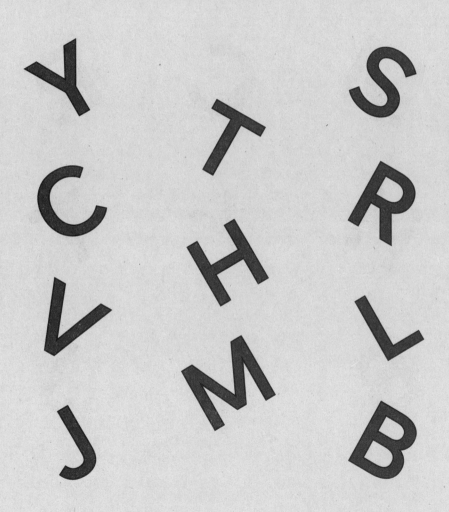

Study the building blocks below until you are familiar with them, then turn the page.

Which two of these did you see? When you think you have the answer, turn back the page to see if it is correct.

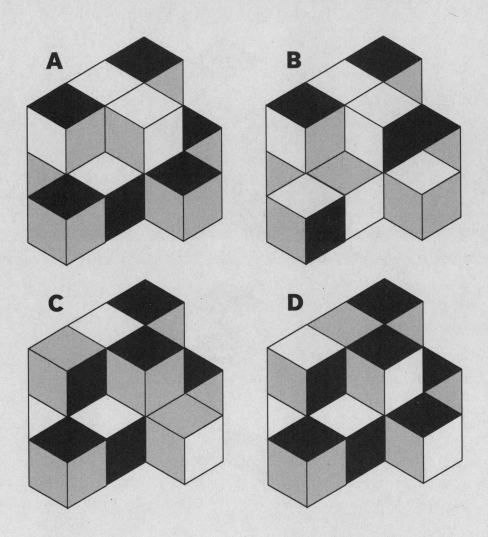

A    B

C    D

Study and memorize the elements below, then turn the page.

| | |
|---|---|
| ARGON | LEAD |
| BARIUM | MERCURY |
| BISMUTH | NICKEL |
| BORON | OXYGEN |
| CARBON | RADIUM |
| COPPER | RHODIUM |
| GOLD | STRONTIUM |
| IRON | ZINC |

Can you find the words in the grid below? Words may run either forwards or backwards, in either a horizontal, vertical, or diagonal direction, but always in a straight line.

```
D R M H E X N R F E Y X I
L Z T D V G T O A I U F T
O N E O L E A D R D H S R
G N O B R A C J M O I L V
I B Z S U T D O Y N B U B
J A S I R T Q R P B P I M
O R A T N A U V G P S Q N
G I U D R C V A M M E O X
J U N L R O Z O U A R R N
B M O E N T N T G I F O M
S F M Y G I H T S L G R J
M C L H C Y Z S I R S D B
G O K K Z O X K A U D J D
L L E M U I D O H R M D I
G L C R Y E H B X T C V W
```

200

Study the arrows below until you are familiar
with them, then turn the page.

Which two arrows have rotated 180 degrees? When you think you have the answer, turn back the page to see if it is correct.

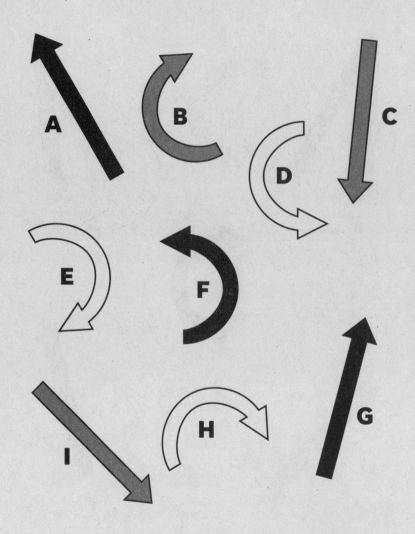

Study and memorize the moonlit scene below, then turn the page.

See how much you can remember about the picture.

# How many bats are flying directly in front of the moon?

5

6

7

9

Study the designs below until you are familiar
with them, then turn the page.

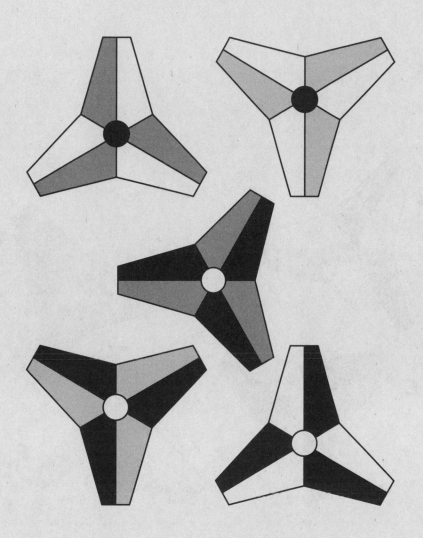

Which new design has appeared? When you think you have the answer, turn back the page to see if it is correct.

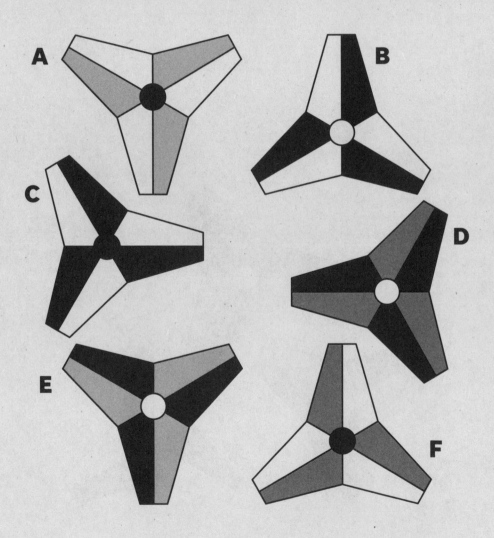

Study the hot-air balloons below until you are familiar with them, then turn the page.

Which two hot-air balloons have changed places? When you think you have the answer, turn back the page to see if it is correct.

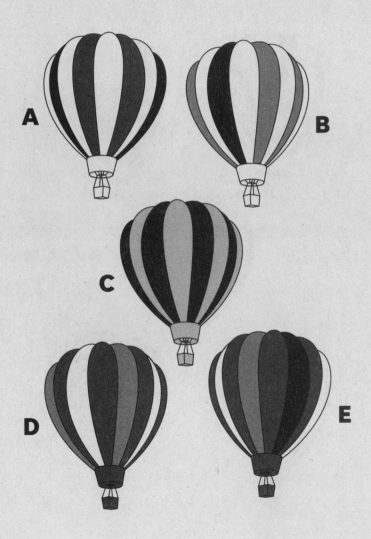

Study and memorize the fish below, then turn the page.

| | |
|---|---|
| ANCHOVY | PORBEAGLE |
| CUTTLEFISH | SALMON |
| DOGFISH | SHARK |
| HERRING | STURGEON |
| MACKEREL | TROUT |
| MARLIN | TUNA |
| PIKE | TURBOT |
| PLAICE | WHALE |

Can you find the words in the grid below? Words may run either forwards or backwards, in either a horizontal, vertical, or diagonal direction, but always in a straight line.

```
A N O E G R U T S B Y N P
C N K H C O N V F Q A I P
J I C E T I H O K K M L M
P L J H L U A P M Q B R U
T E G L O B S L Y L D A L
R R W T X V W D P W A M B
O E J T Q R Y O T Y F S X
U K W W X E B G K U H T F
T C W K L D J F Y R N C I
T A T A E C E I Z R A A J
U M H B T E L S D Q N H C
R W L N Z T B H O O L P S
B R K E L G A E B R O P M
O H S I F E L T T U C R Q
T S D S H Q H E R R I N G
```

Study the houses below until you are familiar
with them, then turn the page.

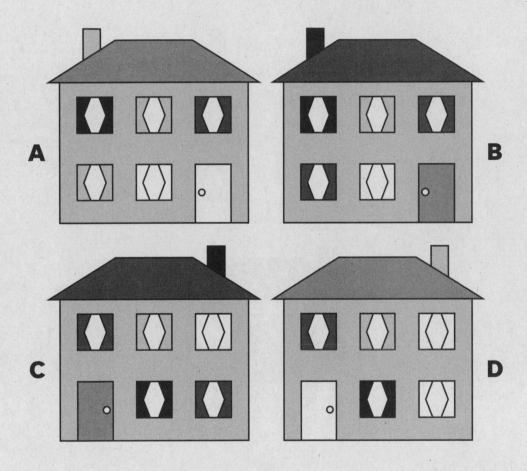

A

B

C

D

USA TODAY

Which house is missing? When you think you have the answer, turn back the page to see if it is correct.

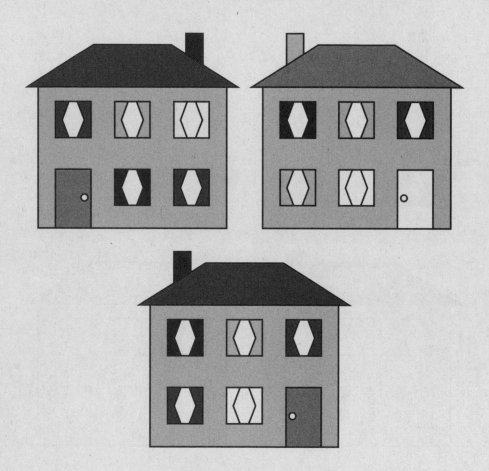

Study and memorize the plane below, then turn the page.

See how much you can remember about the picture.

# What numbers are not displayed on the plane's fuselage?

12

13

14

16

18

Study the boards below until you are familiar
with them, then turn the page.

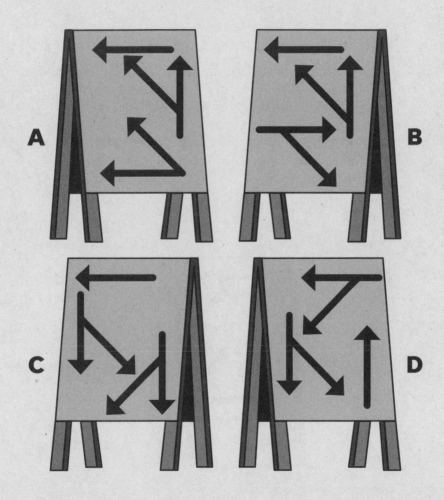

Which board is missing? When you think you have the answer, turn back the page to see if it is correct.

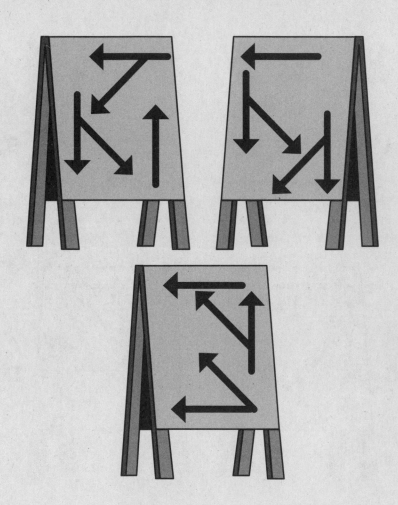

# LEVEL 5

> "It is necessary to relax your muscles when you can. Relaxing your brain is fatal."
>
> —Stirling Moss, Formula 1 racing driver

Well done for reaching level 5. In this section you'll find the most demanding puzzles yet. However, having worked your way through the levels up to this point you will have now established your own methods and tricks for solving the different puzzle types within, so you should be ready for the challenge!

## Memory Facts and Tips

The food we eat can have a major impact on our brains. Keeping a healthy diet and staying hydrated while cutting down high-sugar, fried, and overly processed foods may play an important role in supporting brain function. Berries, walnuts, leafy greens, and fish are among the most beneficial. Dark chocolate, with a cocoa content of at least 70%, is rich in flavanols that improve working memory and concentration, as well as the rate at which you can process information.

Eat carbohydrates—but remember that all carbohydrates are not equal. Your brain needs glucose, but simple carbohydrates (processed foods) release it too quickly, causing your blood sugar levels to spike and then crash, leading to brain fog. Complex carbohydrates release their glucose slowly. For good thinking, think whole grains, beans, vegetables, and fruit.

USA TODAY

Study the pencils below until you are familiar
with them, then turn the page.

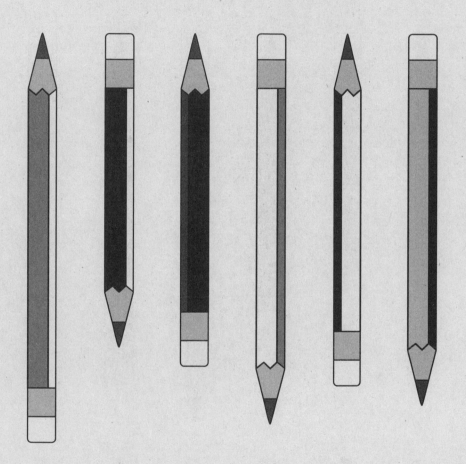

Which two pencils have become shorter? When you think you have the answer, turn back the page to see if it is correct.

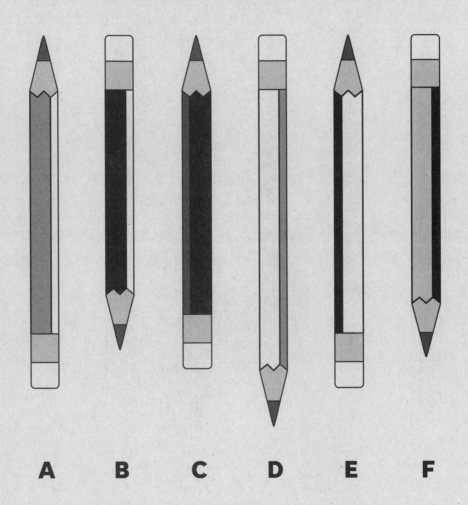

**A    B    C    D    E    F**

Study the cubes below until you are familiar
with them, then turn the page.

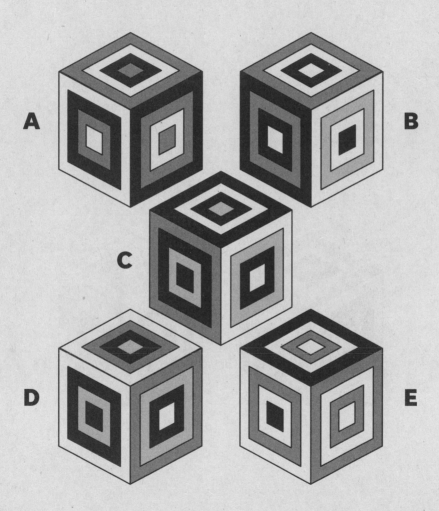

Which cube is missing? When you think you have the answer, turn back the page to see if it is correct.

Study and memorize the sports and games below, then turn the page.

BACKGAMMON      GOLF

BOWLING      QUOITS

BOXING      RACING

CANOEING      SKATING

CHESS      SKIING

CYCLING      SOCCER

DOMINOES      SOFTBALL

FENCING      SWIMMING

FOOTBALL      WRESTLING

Can you find the words in the grid below? Words may run either forwards or backwards, in either a horizontal, vertical, or diagonal direction, but always in a straight line.

```
G N I L T S E R W H G N G
F G G I A M E S A D N G N
O E N N V E R D Z O I N I
O G E I I N H L B M X I L
T H L O T M L B O I O E C
B A C K G A M M O N B W Y
A A P A B G K I J O K S C
L S T T N G G S W E R M Q
L N F I S R N L R S E F Z
G O C A E T I I C H E S S
S A J C L N I I E N D U E
R G C T G I K O C O G I M
I O Y V J U S I U O N I E
S E S A G E N A L Q I A A
F O O T W G S F R J L G C
```

Study the tiles below until you are familiar
with them, then turn the page.

Write in the missing letters and numbers, then turn back the page to see if your answer is correct.

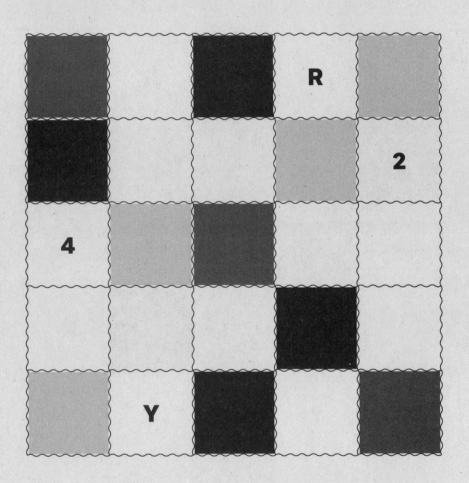

Study and memorize the signpost below, then turn the page.

See how much you can remember about the picture.

# Where is the sign post located?

# How many km is it to Oslo?

# In which city will you be if you travel 8378 km from the signpost?

Study the shapes below until you are familiar
with them, then turn the page.

None has changed position, but four of them each have one extra point. Which one has the same number of points as before? When you think you have the answer, turn back the page to see if it is correct.

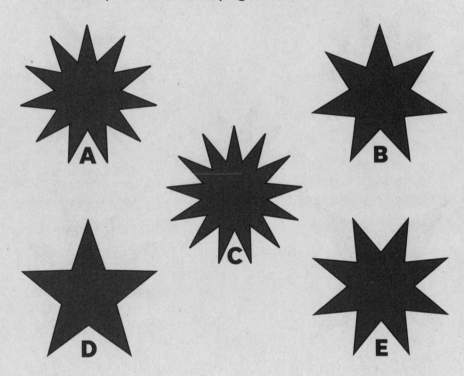

Study the cards below until you are familiar
with them, then turn the page.

Which two cards have changed places? When you think you have the answer, turn back the page to see if it is correct.

Study and memorize the jewels and trinkets
below, then turn the page.

| | |
|---|---|
| BANGLE | CROWN |
| BEADS | CUFFLINK |
| BRACELET | DIADEM |
| BROOCH | LOCKET |
| CAMEO | NECKLACE |
| CHAIN | PEARLS |
| CHARM | PENDANT |
| CHOKER | TIARA |
| CLASP | WATCH |

Can you find the words in the grid below? Words may run either forwards or backwards, in either a horizontal, vertical, or diagonal direction, but always in a straight line.

```
K P T E L E C A R B R Z Y
Z B A Z N Z R H Z T C K O
N G U N P B R O O C H I N
S D A E B E Q B H K M Y O
D P K C L Z N E Y E E V M
U Y R K S G K D D Z H R Y
U Y S L N Z N A A C D K Y
S L R A E P I A T N I N D
O T X C Q D I A B W T I K
C A M E O L W P I P A L I
I R X I M O M A S N J F G
U N O Y U C B R R A J F N
G T W W Y K W O A A L U R
G G F V N E E M S H I C C
T T V A H T N I A H C T X
```

Study the clocks below until you are familiar
with them, then turn the page.

Draw in the four missing hands. When you think you have the answer, turn back the page to see if it is correct.

Study and memorize the elevator buttons
below, then turn the page.

 USA TODAY

See how much you can remember about the picture.

# Which floors have their buttons on the left-hand side of the panel?

# Odds

# Evens

# What is the sum total of the numbers on the elevator buttons displayed?

Study the beach umbrellas below until you are familiar with them, then turn the page.

Which new umbrella has appeared? When you think you have the answer, turn back the page to see if it is correct.

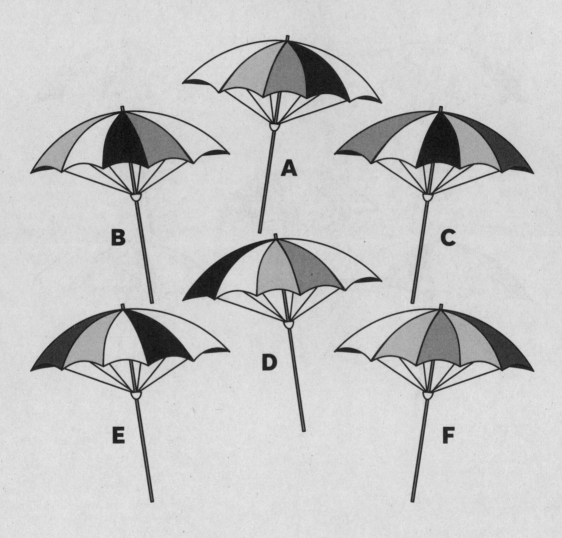

Study the balloons below until you are familiar
with them, then turn the page.

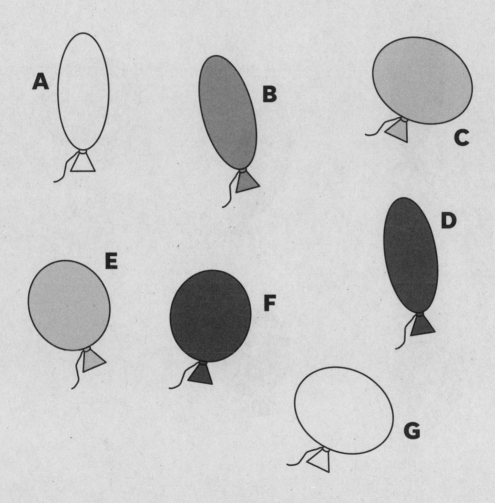

Which balloon is missing? When you think you have the answer, turn back the page to see if it is correct.

Study and memorize the languages below, then turn the page.

| | |
|---|---|
| ARABIC | GREEK |
| CHINESE | HEBREW |
| CROATIAN | ITALIAN |
| DANISH | JAPANESE |
| ENGLISH | LATIN |
| ESPERANTO | MANDARIN |
| FRENCH | POLISH |
| GAELIC | SPANISH |
| GERMAN | SWAHILI |

Can you find the words in the grid below? Words may run either forwards or backwards, in either a horizontal, vertical, or diagonal direction, but always in a straight line.

```
L E G W E R B E H S W I O
V A A X G R O U X P M L R
E H E B R A S A R A B I C
S D L R E E G D N N M P E
P A I P E J N A U I M O S
E N C T K L I G X S T L E
R I I N A T C H L H E I N
A S N T A L I H H I U S A
N H I O N P I C I U S H P
T N R E R A N A H N D H A
O C A P N E M E N P E Y J
E V D N R Q W R E Q F S Y
R W N F E Y R H E C O R E
L F A D C K K F L G H O N
Q J M Z E S W A H I L I C
```

Study the buttons below until you are familiar
with them, then turn the page.

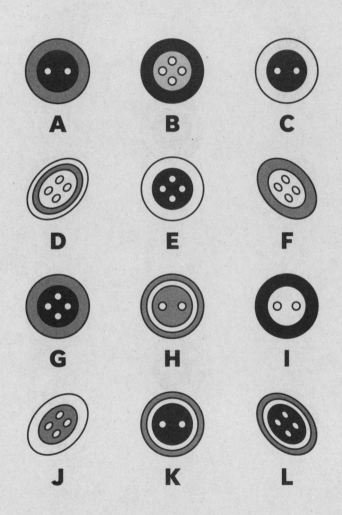

Which two buttons are missing? When you think you have the answer, turn back the page to see if it is correct.

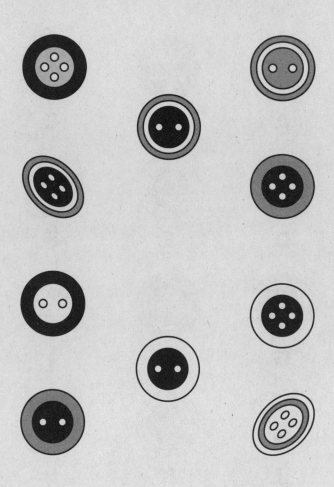

Study and memorize the telephone keypad
below, then turn the page.

See how much you can remember about the picture.

# How would you spell out the word "TELEPHONE" using the numbered keypad?

Study the letters below until you are familiar
with them, then turn the page.

Which three letters have changed shade? When you think you have the answer, turn back the page to see if it is correct.

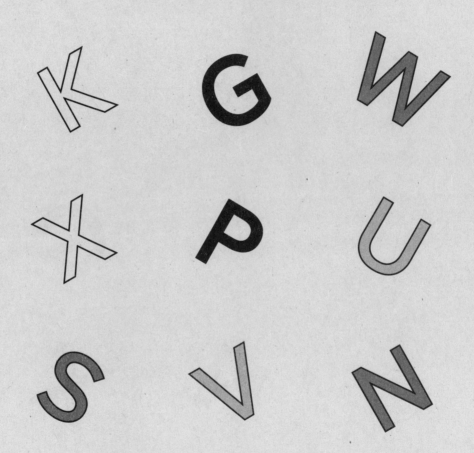

Study the building blocks below until you are familiar with them, then turn the page.

Which new set of building blocks has appeared? When you think you have the answer, turn back the page to see if it is correct.

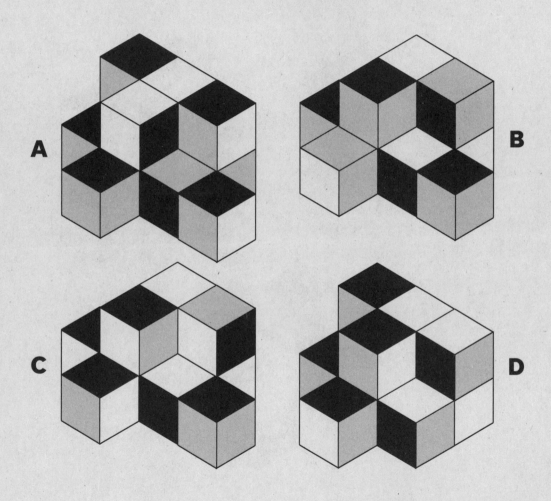

Study and memorize the words relating to butterflies and moths below, then turn the page.

| | |
|---|---|
| ATLAS BLUE | LARVA |
| BRIMSTONE | MONARCH |
| BUTTERFLY | MOTH |
| CARDINAL | PEACOCK |
| CATERPILLAR | RED ADMIRAL |
| CHRYSALIS | SKIPPER |
| COMMA | SWALLOWTAIL |
| EMPEROR | VICEROY |
| GHOST | VOGEL'S BLUE |

Can you find the words in the grid below? Words may run either forwards or backwards, in either a horizontal, vertical, or diagonal direction, but always in a straight line.

```
S E U L B S L E G O V O M
I R S W A L L O W T A I L
L A N I D R A C D L D G U
A L V B V X E M P E R O R
S L V R G N K V H U F Q T
Y I W I A R X T B L X E R
R P K M H L O L U B H E X
H R C S Z M H K U S D X Y
C E O T R J H T E A A Q O
A T C O G E T C D L U N R
M A A N Q E P M R T Q T E
M C E E R X I P R A S T C
O N P F L R P D I O N M I
C B L A A B T D H K W O V
M Y Z L A E N G G A S Y M
```

Study the arrows below until you are familiar
with them, then turn the page.

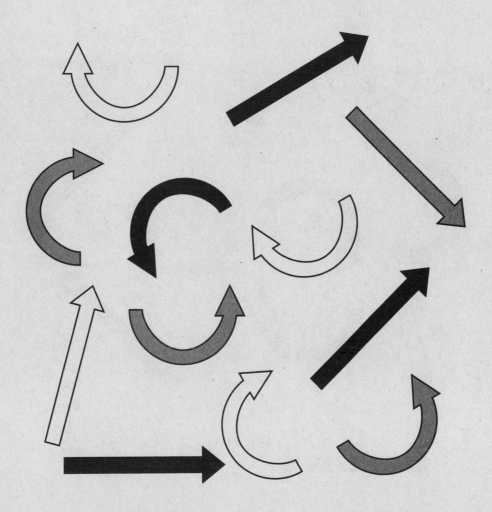

Which three arrows have changed shade? When you think you have the answer, turn back the page to see if it is correct.

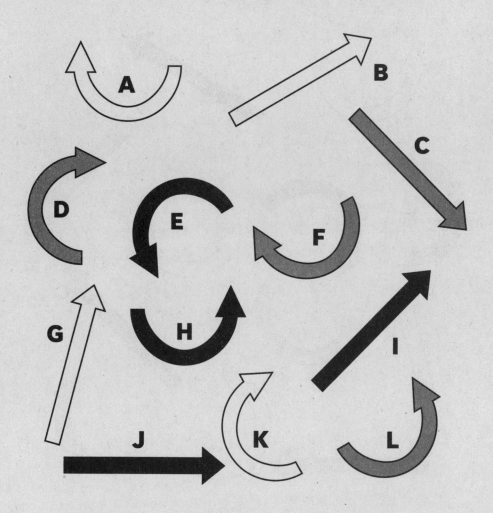

Study and memorize the train timetable below, then turn the page.

See how much you can remember about the picture.

# If you wanted to catch the 419, at what time would you be leaving?

## 4:18 p.m.

## 8:10 a.m.

## 6:20 p.m.

## 5:47 a.m.

## 8:24 a.m.

# If you add together the four train numbers, what is the total?

Study the designs below until you are familiar
with them, then turn the page.

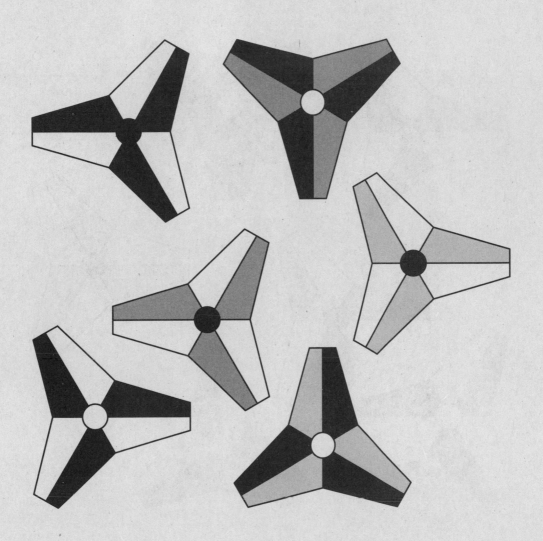

# USA TODAY

Which design has rotated 180 degrees? When you think you have the answer, turn back the page to see if it is correct.

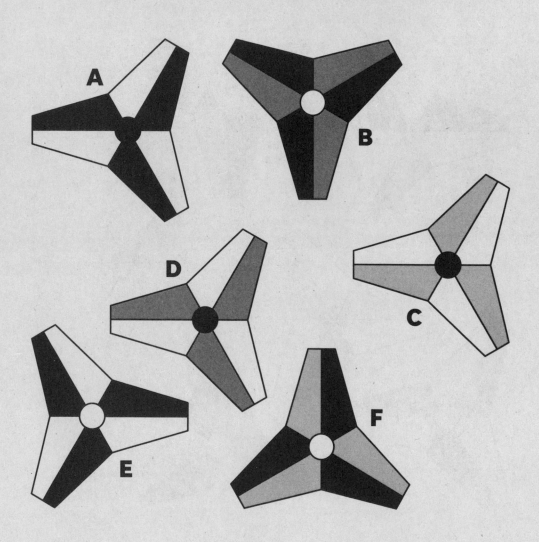

260

Study the hot-air balloons below until you are familiar with them, then turn the page.

Which three hot-air balloons have changed position? When you think you have the answer, turn back the page to see if it is correct.

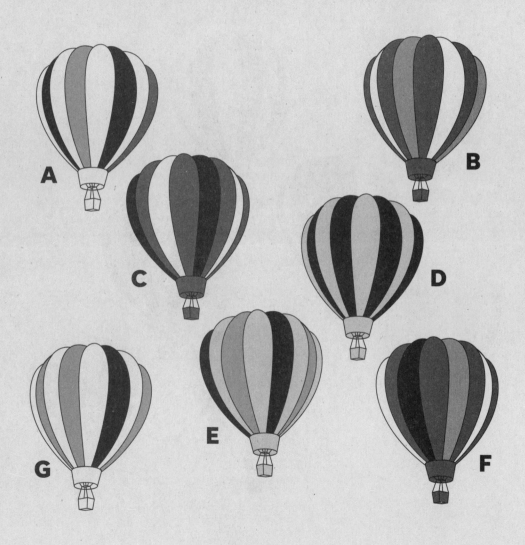

Study the houses below until you are familiar
with them, then turn the page.

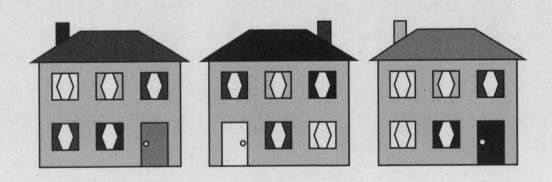

Which two houses have changed position? When you think you have the answer, turn back the page to see if it is correct.

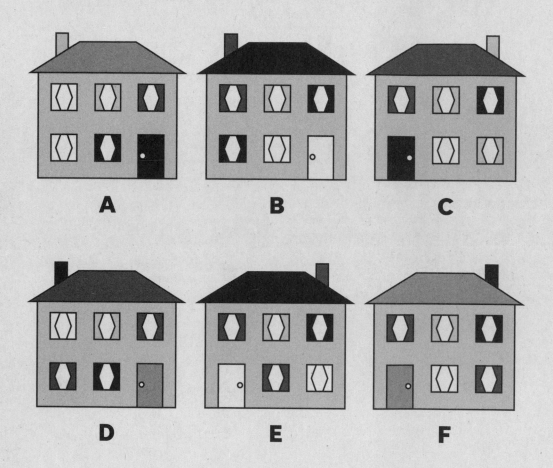

Study and memorize the coins below, then turn the page.

See how much you can remember about the picture.

# When was the bottom right-hand coin minted?

# What country does the middle right-hand coin come from?

## Nicaragua

## Bolivia

## Costa Rica

## Paraguay

Study the boards below until you are familiar
with them, then turn the page.

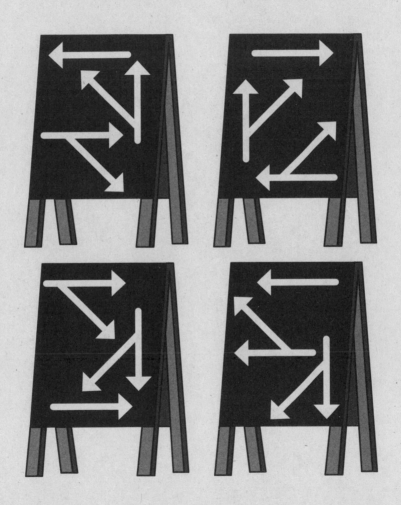

Which board is different? When you think you have the answer, turn back the page to see if it is correct.

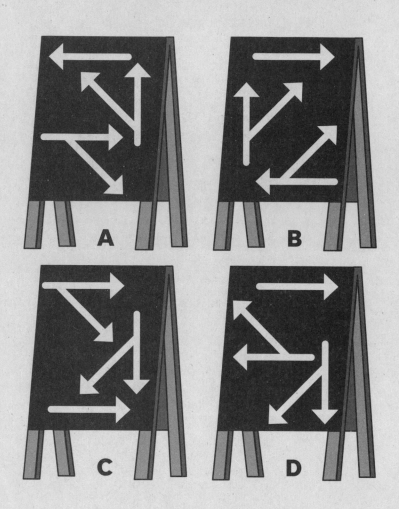

# SOLUTIONS

## LEVEL 1

**Page 3, Pencils**
C

**Page 5, Cube**
A

**Page 7, Word Search – Fruits**

**Page 9, Tiles**
B

**Page 11, Photographic – Transmission Tower**
There are three crossarms on the transmission tower.
There are more than 15 power lines in the picture.

**Page 13, Shapes**
D

**Page 15, Cards**
Six of diamonds

## USA TODAY

**Page 17, Word Search – Colors**

**Page 19, Clocks**
E

**Page 21, Photographic – Umbrellas**
There are 12 umbrellas in the picture.
None are open.

**Page 23, Umbrellas**
B

**Page 25, Balloons**
D

**Page 27, Word Search – Puzzles**

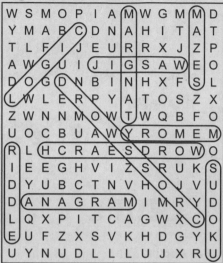

**Page 29, Buttons**
E

**Page 31, Photographic – Chessboard**
White—There are 14 black and 15 white
pieces on the board.
White has both rooks still in their
starting positions.

**Page 33, Numbers**
7 and 5

**Page 35, Building Blocks**
B

## Page 37, Word Search – Weather

## Page 47, Word Search – Toys

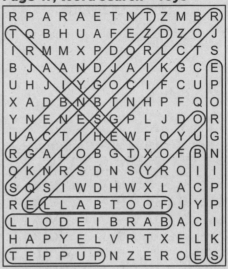

**Page 39, Arrows**

E

**Page 41, Photographic – Ferris Wheel**

There are eight cars partially or wholly visible on the Ferris wheel.

**Page 43, Designs**

B and C

**Page 45, Hot-Air Balloons**

B

**Page 49, House**

A

**Page 51, Photographic – Ship**

The ship has six sails.
The flag of the USA is being flown on the ship.

**Page 53, Board**

A

# LEVEL 2

**Page 57, Pencils**

D

**Page 59, Cubes**

A and C

**Page 61, Word Search – Gemstones**

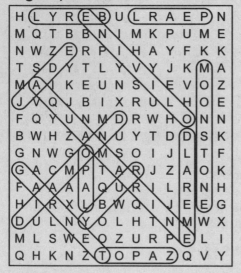

**Page 63, Tiles**

D

**Page 65, Photographic – Chessboard**

There are two knights in the image. Yes, the king is the tallest chess piece and often has a cross on top—the white king is visible on the board.

**Page 67, Shapes**

A

**Page 69, Cards**

Five of spades

**Page 71, Word Search – Tools**

**Page 73, Clocks**

B and D

**Page 75, Photographic – Eiffel Tower**

Four bridge arches can be seen. A carousel can be seen at the bottom right of the Eiffel Tower.

**Page 77, Umbrellas**

A

**Page 79, Balloons**

B

## Page 81, Word Search – Birds

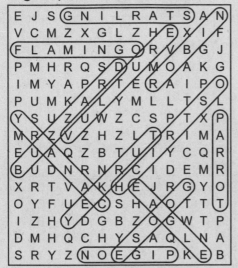

## Page 91, Word Search – Cakes

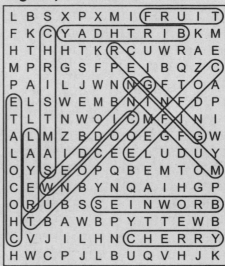

### Page 83, Buttons
C

### Page 85, Photographic – Telephone Keypad
The letters JKL appear on the 5 key.

### Page 87, Letters
Z

### Page 89, Building Blocks
B

### Page 93, Arrows
D and E

### Page 95, Photographic – Bus Stop
If you caught the Q32 bus, you would be going to Jackson Heights.

### Page 97, Designs
C

### Page 99, Hot-Air Balloons
D

### Page 101, Word Search – Clothing

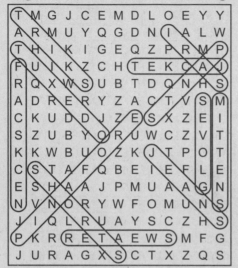

### Page 103, Houses

B

### Page 105, Photographic – Juggling

There are six pieces of fruit in the image—don't forget the one he isn't juggling with!

### Page 107, Boards

C

# LEVEL 3

### Page 111, Pencils

C

### Page 113, Cubes

B

### Page 115, Word Search – European Countries

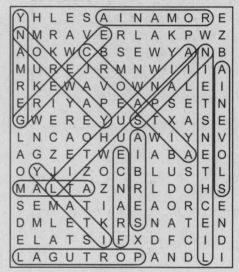

### Page 117, Tiles

B and C

### Page 119, Photographic – Fishes

The two prices not displayed are 4.20 and 5.60.

### Page 121, Shapes

E

### Page 123, Cards

The four, from hearts to spades

### Page 125, Word Search – Wild Flowers

### Page 127, Clocks

D

### Page 129, Photographic – Bridge

Six lanterns light the bridge. Padlocks are attached to the bridge— if you look closely, you can see them along the rails at each side.

### Page 131, Umbrellas

A and C

### Page 133, Balloons

E

### Page 135, Word Search – Cat Breeds

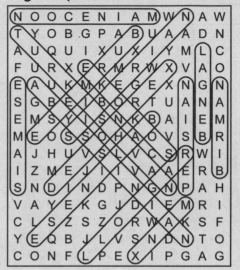

### Page 137, Buttons

I

### Page 139, Photographic – Warehouse

The barrels are six stacks high at their highest point.

### Page 141, Numbers

4

### Page 143, Building Blocks

C

### Page 145, Word Search – Animals

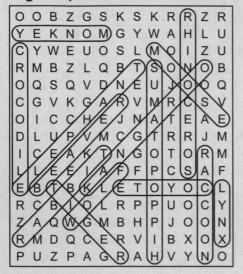

### Page 155, Word Search - Desserts

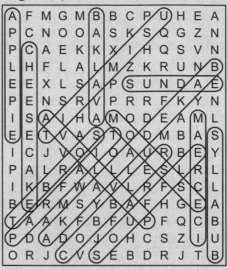

### Page 147, Arrows

G

### Page 157, Houses

C

### Page 149, Photographic – Castle Gate

There are 32 square holes in the closed part of the gate (eight rows and four columns).

### Page 159, Photographic – Sale

The two statements that do not appear on any sign in the store are: NO EXIT and
ANY GARMENT ON THIS RACK $25.55.

### Page 151, Designs

B and D

### Page 161, Boards

B

### Page 153, Hot-Air Balloons

E

# LEVEL 4

### Page 165, Pencils
A and D

### Page 167, Cubes
D

### Page 169, Word Search – US States

### Page 171, Tiles

### Page 173, Photographic – Palm Trees
Nine palm trees can be seen on the traffic island in the foreground.
Yes, vehicles can be seen at the far end of the road on the left–hand side.

### Page 175, Shapes
C and H

### Page 177, Cards
Five of diamonds

### Page 179, Word Search – Shells
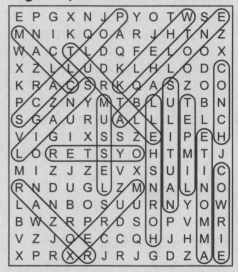

### Page 181, Clocks
C, D, and E

### Page 183, Photographic – Harbor
There are 17 water vessels to be seen in their entirety in the bottom section—don't forget the one that isn't in the water to the right of the image!

### Page 185, Umbrellas
E

### Page 187, Balloons
C and D

## Page 189, Word Search – Dances

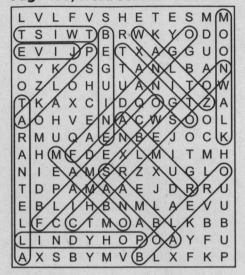

## Page 199, Word Search – Elements

### Page 191, Buttons
D and H

### Page 193, Photographic – Columns
No—the seventh column is mostly out of shot, none of its shadow can be seen.

### Page 195, Letters
S and V

### Page 197, Building Blocks
A and C

### Page 201, Arrows
B and E

### Page 203, Photographic – Moonlit Scene
There are nine bats flying directly in front of the moon.

### Page 205, Designs
C

### Page 207, Hot-Air Balloons
D and E

### Page 209, Word Search – Fish

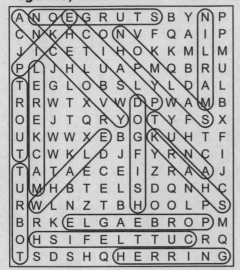

### Page 211, Houses

D

### Page 213, Photographic – Plane

The numbers 12, 16, and 18 are not displayed on the plane's fuselage.

### Page 215, Boards

B

# LEVEL 5

### Page 219, Pencils

A and F

### Page 221, Cubes

B

### Page 223, Word Search – Sports and Games

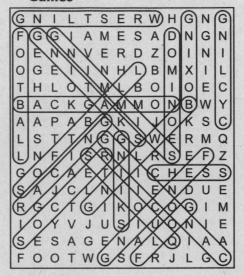

### Page 225, Tiles

### Page 227, Photographic – Signpost

The signpost is located in Svalbard. It is 2046 km to Oslo.
You will be in Bangkok if you travel 8378 km from the signpost.

### Page 229, Shapes

E

### Page 231, Cards

The queen of diamonds and the queen of hearts

## Page 233, Word Search – Jewels and Trinkets

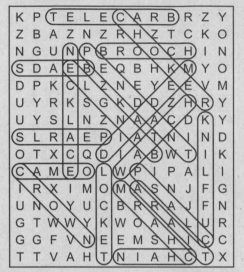

## Page 235, Clocks

## Page 237, Photographic – Elevator Buttons

Even numbers are on the left-hand side of the panel.
The sum total of the elevator buttons is 125 (8+9+10+11+12+13+14+15+16+17).

## Page 239, Umbrellas

C

## Page 241, Balloons

G

## Page 243, Word Search – Languages

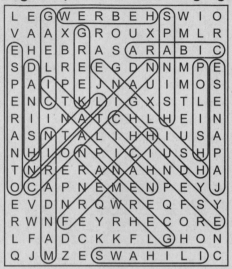

## Page 245, Buttons

F and J

## Page 247, Photographic – Telephone Keypad

Press 8 once for T, 3 twice for E, 5 three times for L, 3 twice for E, 7 once for P, 4 twice for H, 6 three times for O, 6 twice for N, and finally 3 twice for E.

## Page 249, Letters

G, W, and X

## Page 251, Building Blocks

C

280

# USA TODAY

### Page 253, Word Search – Butterflies and Moths

### Page 255, Arrows

B, F, and H

### Page 257, Photographic – Train Timetable

If you wanted to catch the 419, you would be leaving at 8:10 a.m.
If you add together the four train numbers that are completely visible, the total is 1,559 (508+316+419+316).

### Page 259, Designs

C

### Page 261, Hot-Air Balloons

B, E, and G

### Page 263, Houses

A and F

### Page 265, Photographic – Coins

The bottom right-hand coin was minted in 1972.
The middle right-hand coin comes from Costa Rica.

### Page 267, Boards

D

## Play these other great puzzle books by USA TODAY:

*USA TODAY Sudoku*

*USA TODAY Everyday Sudoku*

*USA TODAY Crossword*

*USA TODAY Logic Puzzles*

*USA TODAY Jumbo Puzzle Book 2*

*USA TODAY Picture Puzzles Across America*

*USA TODAY Word Finding Frenzy*

*USA TODAY Sudoku 2*

*USA TODAY Crossword 2*

*USA TODAY Logic 2*

*USA TODAY Sudoku 3*

*USA TODAY Crossword 3*

*USA TODAY Word Roundup*

*USA TODAY Crossword Super Challenge*

*USA TODAY Sudoku Super Challenge*

*USA TODAY Logic Super Challenge*

*USA TODAY Jumbo Puzzle Book Super Challenge*

*USA TODAY Sudoku Super Challenge 2*

*USA TODAY Crossword Super Challenge 2*

*USA TODAY Jumbo Puzzle Book Super Challenge 2*

*USA TODAY Logic Super Challenge 2*

*USA TODAY Sudoku Super Challenge 3*

*USA TODAY Crossword Super Challenge 3*

*USA TODAY Logic Super Challenge 3*

*USA TODAY Jumbo Puzzle Book Super Challenge 3*

*USA TODAY Sudoku and Variants Super Challenge*

*USA TODAY Word Fill-in Super Challenge*

*USA TODAY Teatime Crosswords*

*USA TODAY Sunshine Sudoku*

*USA TODAY Jazzy Jumbo Puzzle Book*

*USA TODAY Lazy Day Logic*

*USA TODAY Large-Print Word Search*